LIVING
TREASURES

LIVING TREASURES

AN ODYSSEY THROUGH CHINA'S EXTRAORDINARY NATURE RESERVES

TANG XIYANG

BANTAM BOOKS, INC. NEW YORK/NEW WORLD PRESS, BEIJING

TORONTO • NEW YORK • LONDON • SYDNEY • AUCKLAND

LIVING TREASURES

A Bantam Book / December 1987

*This book is co-published by Bantam Books, Inc.,
and New World Press.*

All rights reserved.
Copyright © 1987 by Bantam Books, Inc., and New World Press.
Book design by Barbara N. Cohen.
Photo layout by Lurelle Cheverie.
This book may not be reproduced in whole or in part, by
mimeograph or any other means, without permission.
For information address: Bantam Books, Inc.

Library of Congress Cataloging-in-Publication Data

Tang, Xiyang.
  Living treasures.

  1. Natural areas—China.   2. Natural history—China.
3. China—Description and travel—1976–   . I. Title.
QH77.C6T36   1987   508.51   87-47583
ISBN 0-553-05236-5

Published simultaneously in the United States and Canada

PRINTED IN THE UNITED STATES OF AMERICA

WAK   0 9 8 7 6 5 4 3 2 1

CONTENTS

FOREWORD

China is known throughout the world for its vast territory, abounding in natural resources, a source of great pride to the Chinese people. Almost three hundred nature reserves established in recent years have attracted much interest in particular, both in China and overseas. These reserves represent all kinds of well-preserved, primitive ecosystems containing rare animals, plants, and other natural relics, some unique to China. They embody the truth, goodness, and beauty of the natural world. Particularly in these times, when population growth and technological progress pose an increasingly serious threat to natural resources and the environment, nature reserves manifest the harmonious coexistence of man and nature. They are the cradle in which man can dream of his past, the model for the future that man is pursuing. More and more people are seeking a green environment where they can escape from noisy, polluted, crowded cities and parched and dying deserts.

China's nature reserves are in a period of vigorous development. One hundred and seventy new reserves have been created in the last three years—nearly as many as all those established in the last thirty years. In the expansion there are inevitable elements of naïveté and crudeness, and there still remain many problems in both the theory and practice of nature-reserve construction that need to be studied and solved. This is long-term work that will be of vital importance to later generations, and the people of China and the rest of the world hope to make this historical contribution.

The popularization of scientific knowledge about nature reserves is an important task. The author of this book is a member of the educational organ of the China Wildlife Protection Association, as well as a highly experienced journalist and writer of popular science. He visited many nature reserves to collect firsthand materials and scientific information and has combined reportage with science to create his own style of writing, rich in scientific fact yet suited to the tastes of the modern reader and the interests of the tourist.

The vivid photographs in this book make it as expansive, rich, beautiful, and fascinating as nature itself. I thoroughly recommend it to all nature lovers and specialists, young and old, as an excellent guide to the love of nature, science, and today's world; and to workers in the field of nature protection as a vivid and innovative textbook.

—Dong Zhiyong
Vice-President
China Wildlife Protection Association

DISTRIBUTION OF CHINA'S RARE AND PRECIOUS ANIMALS

Map supplied by New World Press, Beijing

FOREWORD

The awakening of China to the western world continues apace. From the earliest years, everything from human contacts to the discovery of the fauna and flora of this vast subcontinent has excited Westerners and foreigners from every part of the rest of the developed world. The new awakening which has come since the 1970's has provided revelation upon revelation for scientists, for informed laymen, and for ardent travelers as well. Finding out about the status of rare species and the extent of the Chinese government's commitment to preserving them and the environment are matters of vital interest and enormous importance to us all.

In *Living Treasures* Tang Xiyang enthusiastically depicts the natural wonders of his country and speaks of the growing awareness of large numbers of people to the need to protect them. This is welcome news, indeed; it encourages us in the outside world who are concerned about the international effects of all preservation efforts in all environments. From this book and a few recent cooperative ventures with international scientific and academic groups, we can take heart about the prospects for increased conservation consciousness in the People's Republic of China.

Certainly Tang Xiyang makes us believe there is progress, and progress is what is desperately needed . . . before it is too late.

In his well-written text, Mr. Tang recounts with verve delightful personal descriptions and anecdotes of his experiences from Hainan Island in the tropical zone of southern China to Yunnan with its remaining wild elephants and north to the tundra regions where cranes and wild swans may be found. He divulges information about lone individuals and large institutions battling to preserve and protect what he aptly calls *Living Treasures.* Every one of these efforts is important for it opens a door wider, lets in light to brighten the prospects for total international cooperation in an area which is blameless and unexceptionable, where no secrets are kept for inessential reasons, and where the best efforts of the best minds must be focused on finding solutions to the problems of preserving and protecting. One reads this book as if it were a letter full of glad tidings. It is not only a sincere step in the right direction, but a charming addition to the bookshelves of scientists, environmentalists, travelers, and concerned people everywhere.

—S. Dillon Ripley
Secretary *emeritus*
Smithsonian Institution
Washington, D. C.

ODYSSEY

Early one fall morning, in a virgin forest alive with bird song, I found myself gasping for breath. The mountain air was thin and cold as I worked my way up steep slopes, clutching at bamboo branches and struggling for footholds on tree roots and rock crevices. Despite the physical discomfort, I felt exhilarated and eager to press on, for I had come to the Wolong Nature Reserve in China's Sichuan Province in the hopes of seeing a giant panda in its natural habitat.

I am not a naturalist or a zoologist. I am a journalist, and although I was born in a small town in Hunan Province, I had spent most of my years in the city of Beijing. My career on a newspaper had been interrupted by the "antirightist movement," followed by the social upheaval known as the "cultural revolution." Then in 1980, I was named editorial director of the magazine *Nature.* My trip to "panda land" was but one step in a major new assignment—to explore my country's ever-expanding network of nature reserves.

Some thirty years ago the People's Republic of China made an impressive long-term commitment of resources to establish reserves to protect its vast and diverse treasure-houses of plant and animal life, its complex ecosystems, and its unusual geological sites. China's nature reserves now number more than three hundred and are scheduled to increase to five hundred by the year 2000. These reserves stretch over hundreds of thousands of acres in five different climatic zones, and their staffs are charged with the mission of preserving for all mankind the unique heritage of rare and fascinating animal and plant life within China's borders. I wanted to see these wonders of nature with my own eyes and describe them for readers unable to make the journey for themselves. Thus my odyssey began.

Along the way I encountered daunting weather, impassable roads and paths, heartbreaking setbacks. I was chased by a wild elephant. I had to suffer mosquitoes feasting on my hands so as not to alarm the silver pheasants I had waited hours to photograph. I waded barefoot through a mountain stream aptly named Rough

River. I climbed trails infested with long-noded pit vipers whose poisonous fangs are more than an inch long. I obtained a specimen of a medicinal plant that grows in such out-of-the-way places that even mountain-hopping herbalists hesitate to search for it.

In a region of Xinjiang that is frost-free only twelve days a year, I crawled to the edge of a cliff and looked down on an unspoiled expanse of "swan lakes," whose beauty might have inspired a new ballet. On China's largest freshwater lake I heard the flutelike song of the crane, a bird that has traditionally symbolized good luck and longevity. Where farmers till rice paddies near ancestral graveyards in central China, I shared the trials and triumphs of a family of crested ibises, a bird that only a few years ago was thought to be extinct. Farther south, near the summit of Mount Fanjing, where the last surviving bands of Guizhou golden monkeys roam, I caught a glimpse of the "magic light" that Buddhists once believed could be seen only by those who had done sufficient charitable and pious deeds that they might hope for immortality. In the Yangtze River valley, I encountered the rare reptile that probably gave rise to the myth of the dragon, and on a tropical island off the southern coast of China, I saw how a tree that breeds like a mammal can provide a better bulwark than manmade dikes against the destructive force of a typhoon.

None of these things did I do alone. Everywhere I went I was guided, and educated, by dedicated scientists and naturalists and by local people who felt a close kinship with nature. I spoke to a world-famous ecologist who had watched two giant pandas mate in the wild, and I met a retired forester who now devotes his life to protecting birds whose migrating flocks first darkened the skies 40 million years ago. I interviewed a man who organized three expeditions to one of the most inaccessible places on earth in search of a "living fossil" tree, the Cathay silver fir, which is neither a fir nor a pine but something in between.

It was not a desire for adventure, not mere curiosity that drove me on. Like the survival of the giant panda,

the future of these enchanting spots is far from assured. The encroachments of civilization threaten the sanctity of their borders, the purity of their air and water, the fragile ecosystems that sustain them. I felt the need to try to alert people everywhere to the precarious existence of many rare and precious creatures and to explain the myriad benefits to society, indeed to all mankind, that the preservation of endangered species may bring. For example, if it can be commercially cultivated, the Cathay silver fir may one day support a new timber industry. In another of our forest reserves which has been called a living museum of biology, scientists found a parasitic wasp which may help control an aphid that lays waste to many acres of sugarcane each year. The great numbers of biologically active, medically potent plants in the area known as the "Roof of Central China" have not even been fully catalogued.

But the value to mankind of preserving rare species goes far beyond such applications and catalogues. To discourage the killing of animals that belong to endangered species, the government in certain localities actually compensates farmers for crops damaged by such animals. This policy recognizes that every living creature has something to teach us about the world we live in, including our common past. Nor is this recognition of the interdependence of all life the product of a recent "scientific" insight. In my travels, I came across places where plants and animals have been protected not by the actions of scientists but by local people who acknowledged a duty to preserve the natural wonders around them. The herdsmen of Xinjiang's Yurdus Basin live in peaceful coexistence with the swan, whom they regard as a bearer of good luck from heaven. The Dai people of Yunnan Province venerate the white elephant and the forests they share with this animal. The pilgrims who went to Mount Fanjing centuries ago to pay homage to Buddha also treated with respect the natural treasures they found there. In such places, today's nature reserves have simply inherited the work of preservation begun so honorably by those who came before.

In the years I have spent exploring just a few of China's nature reserves, I met a few people who failed to live up to this tradition of guardianship, but they were exceptions. In general, the people I met inspired in me a new appreciation of man's place in nature. The more I saw of life in the wild, the more I desired to see. Not every trip was totally successful. As you will read, I never saw the reclusive giant panda, although I had the privilege of hearing a panda cub cry. But I shall never forget the feeling that came to me on that cold fall morning as I followed the steep upward trail of the giant panda through a virgin forest ringing with birdsong. After spending most of my life in the city, I felt that at long last I had come home.

AN ENDANGERED TREASURY OF MEDICINAL HERBS

In Chinese, *shen nong* means "divine peasant." According to legend, Shen Nong was an emperor and teacher of husbandry and traditional medicine in ancient China, said to have lived in about 2838 B.C. In order to cure one of his people, he went to a high, steep mountain to search for a rare and precious herb that was supposed to grow on sheer cliffs and precipices. He cut down many tall trees and built a scaffold so he could climb the mountain. Since then the place has been called Shennongjia—Shen Nong's Scaffold.

Ancient books mention the existence of Shen Nong. In the *Huainanzi* (a classic of the Han Dynasty, 206 B.C.–A.D. 220, believed to be the work of Liu An, Prince of Huainan) it is written that Shen Nong "tasted hundreds of herbs himself and drank the water from many springs and wells so that people might know which were sweet and which were bitter. On some days Shen Nong tasted as many as seventy poisonous herbs."

The earliest extant Chinese pharmacopoeia, known as *Shen Nong's Canon of Herbs,* included 365 medicinal herbs, most of which, it is said, Shen Nong had tasted himself. There is no way of finding out whether the amazing Shen Nong was a real man, a symbol of a clan, or the personification of the human desire to heal the ill and wounded and to rescue the dying. While Shen Nong may be a mystery, there is no question about why the legend is set in Hubei Province rather than elsewhere. Medicinal plants grow there in astonishing variety and abundance; there is also a rich supply of medicinal herbs that are rare in all other parts of the country, and the local people take advantage of these gifts of nature. Their collection and cultivation of herbs and plants are second in economic importance only to the production of grain crops. There, too, the unique tradition of Chinese herbal medicine flourishes. (Plants can be used as medicine because in the course of their metabolic life they produce a great variety of substances beneficial to human health. For example, there are thousands of physiologically active alkaloids, and each alkaloid acts as a depressant or stimulant to a given function of the hu-

man body.) The practitioners of herbal medicine possess a vast store of pharmacological and medical knowledge that has yet to be rigorously studied and fully exploited.

Why is Shennongjia so rich in medicinal plants and herbs? The thousands of different plants and herbs produced in the area require such a wide variety of geographic and climatic conditions that one can scarcely believe it possible for all of them to come from the same place. Some grow only in high mountains, others in deep valleys; some need a hot dry climate, others a cool wet one; some thrive on rocky precipices, others in clear streams; some must coexist with a particular animal, plant, moss, fungus, lichen, or alga.

Clearly, I had to travel through Shennongjia and see for myself its astounding diversity. So I visited many different parts of the region. I went to the fifty-mile-long Hou River, which flows through the region, and I visited the fathomless Swallow's Cave, Badong Pass, with its view of Sichuan Province, and the picturesque Hongping Long Corridor. I descended to Sun Bay at an altitude of 1,378 feet and ascended to Unnamed Peak at 10,184 feet above sea level.

THE ROOF OF CENTRAL CHINA

From Unnamed Peak we looked down at the "Roof of Central China." What we saw was entirely different from the complex vegetation growing farther below. Here, three kinds of plants greeted the eye: Tract upon tract of arrow bamboo danced in the wind like a solid ocean reaching far to the horizon, and on this ocean red clouds drifted. No! They were alpine rhododendrons bursting with joy. Against this light-red and pale-green background, clusters of firs stood tall and straight. Dressed in green, they unfurled their bannerlike crowns along

the rocks in the mountain breeze—undaunted mountaineers, braving the cold, swinging their arms as they marched briskly upward. They really are champion mountaineers, for they alone ascend to the top, leaving all the other tall trees far behind.

The vast forest looked green and lush. About a billion years ago this was open ocean, but by about 570 million years ago, silt and deposit had gradually transformed it into a shallow sea and seashore. About 70 million years ago the earth underwent a major orogeny—the geologic process of mountain-making by folding of the earth's crust. In this case it was the Himalayan movement, and it gave birth to Shennongjia. Later on, because of yet another orogeny, Shennongjia rose as the highest peak in Central China and is known today as the "Roof of Central China."

The mountains are high and the slopes steep, increasing the erosion levels of the rivers. The result is a great variety of soils, rocks that form sharp vertical angles, and complex land formations and topography. Shennongjia verges on the Yangtze River in the south and on the Han River in the north; in the west it borders on the Daba Mountains and in the east on the Jianghan Plain. Both geographically and climatically it is the transitional zone where East meets West, and North meets South. Because of its dangerous topography, the area is sparsely populated and much of it is covered with forest. Rainfall is plentiful and the climate is quite unusual. One can experience all four seasons at once. The local people say, "At the foot of the mountain it is midsummer; in the mountain valley it is spring; halfway up the mountain the trees are in their autumn colors, while the mountaintop is covered with snow. Red, orange, yellow, green, blue, and purple; spring, summer, autumn, and winter are all merged in one." All these different factors—historical, geographical, geological, geomorphological, climatological—have endowed Shennongjia with this complex environment of a thousand rocks and gullies, of interlocking mountains and rivers, of drifting clouds and flowing streams, all one majestic spectacle for the eye and a paradise for nearly six hundred species of animals and more than two thousand species of plants, including the medicinal plants.

GOLDEN HAIRPIN AND FLYING SQUIRREL

Two men took me up one of Shennongjia's mountains to gather medicinal herbs. One of the men was a herbalist; the other, a member of the militia. I had expressed only one wish: to collect some golden hairpin *(jinchai)*. I had set my mind on this, not just because golden hairpin sells for 240 yuan (about $60) for half a kilogram (a little over a pound) and was formerly presented as a precious gift to emperors and heads of state, and not just because it was taken by famous opera singers Mei Lanfang and Ma Lianliang to protect their voices,

Golden hairpin

but above all because I had heard all sorts of tales about this herb since I had arrived at Shennongjia. I was told that golden hairpin grows not simply on steep cliffs and precipices, but only within the sound of rippling mountain streams as well. It was said that golden hairpin and the flying squirrel form a pair. The flying squirrel loves the fragrance of golden hairpin, while golden hairpin depends on the flying squirrel's droppings for nutrients. Herbalists have to use ropes to scale the cliffs where the herb grows. To protect the golden hairpin, flying squirrels often bite through the ropes, causing the herbalists to drop to their deaths in the abyss far below. For their own safety, herbalists protect their ropes with bamboo tubes. If all this seems a little farfetched, it does illustrate the difficult ecological environment in which the golden hairpin lives and how hazardous it is to get to it.

We left after breakfast. On his back the herbalist was carrying a thick rope about fifty-five feet long, used especially for collecting golden hairpin. The rope had a piece of red silk tied to one end which was probably meant as a charm to ensure both safety and success in finding what we sought. Soon we were in an enormous, magical garden of herbs. Every few steps the herbalist would bend to pick an herb or dig out a root or stem and show it to me. "Look, this is fritillary [*Fritillaria cirrhosa*]. This is Japanese ginseng [*Panax pseudo-ginseng var. japonicus*]," he would say. I had made the right choice by asking to search for golden hairpin, because where it grows there are many other medicinal plants. "This is anemone [*Anemone hupehensis*]," the herbalist would go on. "This is root of Chinese angelica [*Aralia chinensis*]. This is savior grass [*Potentilla freyniana*]. This is pearl fragrance [*Valeriana officinalis*]."

In less than half an hour I had recorded forty-nine species of medicinal plants in my notebook. Even the air seemed permeated with herbal fragrance. The herbalist told me that because of the abundance of medicinal

Golden monkeys in Shennongjia

herbs in this area, even the honey the bees collect from the flowers has highly medicinal properties. It is known as medicinal honey and is much more expensive than the ordinary variety.

The herbalist was in his thirties—bright, strong, ca-

pable, and most helpful in answering my questions. He told me that the biggest root of Asian bell (*Codonopsis pilosula*) they had ever dug out here was as tall as a man; the biggest root of balloonflower (*Platycodon grandiflorum*) as big as a turnip; and the tubers of one single *Gastrodia elata* could weigh as much as 3.5 to 4 kilograms (7.7 to 8.8 pounds). However, he was not so helpful on the subject of looking further for the golden hairpin. After we had climbed the mountain for two hours, he tried to back out by saying, "It is too far away and too dangerous; you'd better not go there. We can collect some *wee* golden hairpin and *honey* golden hairpin near here; they have about the same properties."

But I obstinately insisted that we press on. "My sole purpose here," I said firmly, "is to see how you collect golden hairpin."

He was not too pleased and retorted, "If golden hairpin were so easy to get at, there wouldn't be any poor people in this world!"

I felt rather hurt, but said resolutely, "Come on! I'll follow you wherever you go."

He realized he could not talk me out of it, so he broke a branch off a tree and started clearing a path in front of us. We hadn't advanced more than three steps when he whipped a snake to death and slung it on a branch, its tail still curling up in convulsions.

We climbed up to the edge of a precipice, and the herbalist said to me in a commanding voice: "You wait for me here." I lay underneath a green pine overhanging the precipice and looked down in cool detachment, but could not help exclaiming, "How beautiful!" It was indeed as someone described:

> Rugged cliffs a thousand feet
> Looking down on a verdant sea.
> Ten thousand fathoms high the pines
> Propping up waves of clouds.

In front of me rose a tall, slender, graceful solitary peak. It looked just like one in a painting, its summit

dotted on either side with a few brushstrokes of dark firs. The peak seemed so close and clear, yet between us were white clouds above and the precipice below. I saw the herbalist on the other side, slipping through the pines and rocks like a monkey. The rope was still tied to his back, which meant there was an even more hazardous path in front of him. Then he disappeared: He had gone behind the peak.

A giant salamander in the Yingu River valley

I waited for a good hour and a half before the herbalist returned, the rope hanging loosely from his shoulder. He looked like a soldier returning from the battlefront. In spite of his great physical strength and exceptional climbing skill, he seemed completely exhausted. He took a golden hairpin from his breast and offered it to me. So I could keep this living specimen longer, he had also cut out the rock on which it was growing. I took it in both hands, saying repeatedly, "Thank you! Oh, thank you!"

For three consecutive years the Wuhan Institute of Botany had explored the plant resources of Shennongjia and compiled a five-hundred-page volume called *The Shennongjia Flora*. For some unknown reason the work does not include the golden hairpin. (The plant belongs to the genus Dendrobium of the family Orchidaceae.) I held this tiny plant in my hands and observed it for a long time, thinking to myself: *This is not merely a rare and precious herbal specimen, but a symbol of victory.*

FROM THE WILD TO THE CULTIVATED *GASTRODIA ELATA*

Among medicinal plants the *Gastrodia elata* is unique. First, it is not an autophyte—that is, it does not use chlorophyll for photosynthesis but depends on engulfing the honey fungus, thus directly absorbing the organic elements of heterotrophic plants. The honey fungus itself is rich in vitamin A, mannitol, and D-threitol, and through the biochemical action of the *Gastrodia elata* it becomes a rare and precious herb, the result of a synthesis of plant and fungus. Second, the mode of nutrition has brought about an ecological variation. Because they lack photosynthetic function, the branches and leaves have gradually lost their purpose and degenerated, producing a rare phenomenon among plants: a bare stem without leaves. Third, because it requires a highly specialized environment—the presence of the honey fungus, decomposed roots of trees, soil with a fairly thick humus, relatively high altitude, and so forth—the *Gastrodia elata* does not multiply easily. It is in short supply, yet much in demand both at home and abroad, so its price has skyrocketed. As a result, resources have

A thousand-year-old David keteleeria

been seriously depleted, and the areas in which it grows have been ravaged. The best solution would be to transform the wild herb into a cultivated one, as has been done with the deerhorn *(Cornu cerri pantotrichum)*, musk *(Moschus)*, ginseng *(Panax ginseng)*, root of Chinese angelica, and other crude drugs. Some drug farms and individual peasant families at Shennongjia have already started experimenting with cultivating the *Gastrodia elata*.

To find out about the cultivation of the *Gastrodia elata* and other medicinal herbs, I visited the Tianjiashan Drug Farm. This is the biggest drug-producing base in the region of Shennongjia. Its four branches are situated at varying altitudes to provide different geographical conditions, so that many kinds of medicinal herbs can be cultivated. They have already successfully cultivated the *Gastrodia elata* and are gradually expanding the area of production.

Communes in the region have also set up more than

A. "A pearl on the head"

B. "Seven leaves and one flower"

C. Shrubbery rhodiola

D. "A bowl of water by the riverside"

E. Japanese ginseng

F. The fruit of the Chinese magnolia vine

G. Chinese herbaceous peony

H. Chinese flowering quince

I. *Acanthopanax setchaenensis*

J. The fruit of a cork tree

K. Clavaria

L. Usnea

M. Woolyfruit stylophorum

thirty drug farms, covering a total area in excess of 2,700 *mu* (about 445 acres). If we add the smaller-scale drug farms of the production brigades, the annual output of medicinal herbs, including goldthread *(Coptis chinensis)*, Chinese angelica, common coltsfoot *(Tussilago farfara)*, fritillary *(Fritillaria cirrhosa)*, root of pubescent angelica *(Angelica pubescens)*, safflower *(Carthamus tinctorius)*, bark of Chinese cork tree *(Phellodendron chinense)*, eucommia bark *(Eucommia ulmoides)*, and stem bark of medicinal magnolia *(Magnolia officinalis)*, amounts to 200 to 250 tons, with a value of about 1 million yuan ($250,000), or one third of the income of its diversified economy. Besides, everyone here—man or woman, old or young—can go up the mountain to collect herbs, so the region of Shennongjia sells almost 500 tons of crude drugs to the state every year.

A PEARL ON THE HEAD

At Shennongjia one hears some quite original names for herbs, such as "a pearl on the head," "a bowl of water by the riverside," and "Prince Wen's pen." The names are very picturesque and easy to remember. The herb most in demand is pearl on the head. It has many properties and can be used as a blood activator, analgesic, hemostatic, antinarcotic, and antirheumatic, and has benevolent curative effects in the treatment of vertigo and headaches, fractures and injuries, high blood pressure, and neurasthenia. People come or write from everywhere to obtain pearl on the head.

It grows at altitudes higher than 6,500 feet above sea level. A perennial herbaceous plant, found in thick grass in forests, pearl on the head has a single upright stem topped by three almost rhomboid-shaped verticillate leaves. In summer a little bright-yellow flower blooms on top of the leaves, and in autumn the plant bears a fruit as big as a pea—hence its name: a pearl on the head. Its scientific name is *Trillium tschonoskii* (meaning "long-

A fir tree and its epiphytical vines on Mount Ba, Shennongjia

life herb"), which reflects its medicinal properties. The part used for medicinal purposes is its rootstock, or rhizome, called "pearl of the earth." Its fruit, called "pearl of heaven," has even greater medicinal qualities but cannot be preserved. The herbalists themselves eat the pearl of heaven and sell the pearl of the earth. The herbalists are said to live long lives, enjoy good health, and scale the cliffs with agility even at advanced ages because they eat the pearl of heaven. The Tianjiashan

A sunbird in Shennongjia Nature Reserve

Drug Farm is also experimenting with the cultivation of pearl on the head, and when I was visiting there, the herb seedlings already had three little leaves, but it was not yet the season for its fruit.

Most of the names of these herbs have been passed down from generation to generation and express their particular characteristics and limitations, but can't be regarded as a system of classification. In general, the names fall into two categories: *qi* and *huanyang*. *Qi* means "seven," as in sheep's-horn seven *(Aconitum hemsleyanum)*; Japanese ginseng, seven big leaves *(Panax pseudo-ginseng* var. *japonicus)*; and white three sevens *(Panax japonicum)*. There are said to be seventy-two sevens, though the number may not be exact but probably just indicates how numerous the sevens are. *Huanyang* means "to restore the *yang*," *yang* being one of the two main elements of Chinese traditional medicine. The thirty-six *huanyangs* include nine deaths *huanyang*, cypress *huanyang*, and golden ear *huanyang*. Sometimes one herbal drug may have many different names. For instance, "seven leaves and one flower," "seven story tower," and "seven conchs" actually all refer to the same plant. The first is its scientific name, the second its traditional Chinese medical term, and the last its herbal name.

Some herbal drugs are potent, some mild; some can even be poisonous if not properly used. We can neither totally accept nor totally reject their medicinal value. At this time, it may be wise to picture herbal medicine and its practitioners as a vast treasure house whose door has only just been opened to biomedical researchers who will reveal its secrets.

Badongya, Shennong Stone Forest

A
VISIT
TO
PANDA
LAND:
SAVING
THE
PANDAS

Ever since 1869, when the first giant panda was shot in Baoxing County, Sichuan Province, the whole world has been panda crazy. So when I heard that a special research center was being set up in Sichuan's Wolong Nature Reserve, the natural habitat of the panda, I set out as soon as I could in the hope of seeing a giant panda in the wild.

I left Chengdu at eight o'clock in the morning with two companions: Hu Jinchu, associate professor of biology at Nanchong Teachers College in Sichuan and deputy leader of the Chinese experts at the Giant Panda Research Center of the China World Wildlife Fund (WWF); and Liu Xianping, a writer from Anhui Province who specializes in biographies of scientists. After driving at full speed through Guan and Wenchuan counties (in a green van emblazoned with the WWF panda emblem), we came to a mountain gorge where the water was an unbelievable sapphire-blue. Hu remarked, "The panda's habitat is always a beauty spot." No wonder, I thought, since the panda's very existence depends on three essentials: high mountains and deep valleys, thick bamboo forests, and rippling streams. I sensed we were approaching the panda's homeland, and sure enough, at the entrance to a very long tunnel I saw the name: Wolong Nature Reserve.

I thought we had reached our destination, but our van sped on for another hour until we reached Wolong Pass. Here we got out, walked across an iron chain bridge spanning the Pitiao River, which we had been following for the past two hours, and began climbing a winding mountain path. It was already getting dark when, three hours later, we finally arrived at the research center's observation post.

The site was chosen because there are large numbers of pandas in the vicinity, its altitude (8,265 feet above sea level) makes it safe from mud and rock slides, and water is readily available. To get to a well, one has only to climb down a path of fifty-one steps; this path gives the observation post its name: Camp 51.

The camp consists of one log cabin and six tents,

where Chinese and foreign experts and staff live and work all year round. Although it occupies little more than a thousand square feet and is scarcely visible until one comes hard upon it, Camp 51 has become world-famous. Chinese and foreign newspapers and magazines report regularly on its activities; and it was from here that the news that Zhen-Zhen had given birth to a cub was proclaimed to the world.

THE FIRST DAY OF EXPLORATION

The next day we rose at dawn to get ourselves ready for the expedition. Hu led the way, with all of us carrying cameras and other equipment for observation, as well as our lunches. The day's program was to traverse a three-hundred-foot gorge, climb to a place called Zhonggang at an altitude of 10,168 feet, make four quadrats (small plots laid out for study—in this case of arrow bamboo), and trace the giant panda's movements on our way.

We were surrounded by virgin forest—soaring firs, spruces, and bronze birches, with vines and bamboo thickets filling in the empty spaces. Lichens and mosses of all colors of the rainbow deepened the air of mystery pervading the forest. Winter was drawing near; fallen leaves and pine needles formed a thick carpet beneath our feet. The first creatures to welcome us were a flock of brilliantly colored pheasants *(Tragopan temminckii)*, which fled as soon as they noticed us. From across the hill birdsong reached us. For me, after living nearly half a century in a city, it was like coming home to Mother Nature—an exhilarating experience.

The going was rough. We clutched at bamboo branches and found footholds on tree roots and rock crevices as we worked our way up the steep slopes and sheer cliffs. At such high altitudes the air was thin, and we gasped for breath as we struggled on. Often we were lucky to find an old tree trunk that would serve as a bridge over a ravine or chasm. Hu told us: "There are seven trails like this around the observation post, with a total length of one hundred kilometers [sixty-two miles]. These are not the trails of hunters, herdsmen, or peasant herb collectors, but the paths we have trod during our four years of observation. Nobody else has ever ventured here." As we listened to him, sweat was running down our backs, and we began to appreciate what it was like to follow in the footsteps of dedicated scientists.

After crossing Niudaopian Gully, we arrived at Zhonggang and watched Hu work on the first quadrat of bamboo. The scientist's job often consists of making simple things extremely complicated. If one were to ask a local villager "What is the life span of the bamboo?" he might answer, "Four to five years." But the scientist seeks a more exact answer through methodical experiment. He slips a numbered red plastic band around a newly sprouted bamboo shoot and observes the bamboo every month until it withers away, carefully recording his observations. As for the relationship between the bamboo and the giant panda, that was what Hu was investigating now.

From an area one meter square (a little larger than a square yard) he cut down all the bamboo stalks—twenty-three samples—and classified them according to age: those that had sprouted this year, those from the year before, those from more than two years ago, and the dead ones. Then he measured their height, weight, and thickness of stem, entering all this information on a form along with the species, climate, and place of collection. If data are collected from hundreds of thousands of specimens at different altitudes in different regions, many important questions can be answered.

For more than ten years Hu has trekked through the high mountains and deep valleys of western Sichuan Province, braving all weather, camping out in the open, staying with the giant pandas day and night. His wife and daughter complain that he has become almost a "savage." Yet this steady, even drudging labor has led to the writing of two major scientific works and a score of articles on the giant panda, for the most part composed on a pad spread across his knees, by the light of an oil lamp in his tent.

After Hu had finished the second quadrat, we unexpectedly came upon the feces of a giant panda. They looked like big turnips and seemed quite fresh. Hu said, "If these aren't today's, they're certainly yesterday's." Exciting news for Liu and me! Perhaps our wish to see the giant panda in its natural surroundings was about to be granted. Hu carefully picked up the feces, measured and weighed them, and put them into a plastic bag which he stowed in his rucksack.

"Please don't confuse them with our lunch!" Liu cautioned.

We all laughed, but Hu replied, "Don't underrate these feces. They can tell us lots of things, such as what kind of bamboo the giant panda likes best, which part of the bamboo he likes, how much of the plant's nutritional value he absorbs, whether he has intestinal parasites, and so on. Pan Wenshi, a lecturer at Beijing University, recently suggested that by measuring the undigested pieces of bamboo, it might be possible to determine the distance between the panda's teeth. Anyway, we wrap up all the feces and send them to Beijing regularly for biochemical analysis. After collecting many feces and analyzing them one by one, we can tell how many giant pandas there are in the region. This is a scientific method of counting the panda population."

As we talked we continued the search. At 8,954 feet, 9,216 feet, and 9,282 feet above sea level we found feces of the same giant panda. We were getting more and more excited.

Although the giant panda has inhabited the earth for some 3 million years, about as long as human beings have, man's exploitation of the earth's resources has forced

Siguniangshan, the highest peak of the Wolong Nature Reserve

the panda to retreat to this diminished area. Pandas are clumsy, unable to catch their own food or fend off enemies. They breed slowly and have been able to survive solely by hiding themselves in these high mountains, deep valleys, thick forests, and bamboo thickets. It's easy enough to see a panda in the zoo, but to view one in its natural habitat is almost impossible.

After the French priest Father David Armand learned of the existence of the giant panda in 1869, foreign hunters, zoologists, tourists, and adventurers traveled to China, sparing neither money nor effort in a race to catch this rare animal. If they could not catch one alive, they would be happy to shoot one or even just to set their eyes on one. However, apart from travelers who bought a few giant-panda skins from Chinese hunters, none of these people so much as glimpsed a panda until 1916, when an Englishman announced that he was "the first white man to see a living panda." Actually, all he had seen was "an animal that resembled a big white ball, sitting in a tree at a distance of about one hundred meters." He had "just caught a glimpse of it, when it disappeared."

How could we hope to encounter, on our first time out, an animal that so many other people had spent so many years trying in vain to see? I knew the odds were against us, yet I could not help hoping.

With our eyes we searched the bamboo thickets and gazed into the trees. We discovered the hoofprints of a takin, a large goat antelope related to the musk ox. Apparently it was following the same trail we were. Hu got a little nervous: "I wouldn't care to meet a takin. They can be very fierce."

Nevertheless, our desire to see the panda overcame all other considerations and we pressed on. I kept thinking how nice it would be to spot a panda resting in a tree. Then we could take our time looking at it and shooting pictures. If we encountered the animal on a narrow path, we might frighten it—and ourselves.

We reached 9,968 feet, higher than the Golden Summit of Mount Emei. We had completed the fourth quadrat without coming across any further traces of the panda. Liu and I could climb no higher, so we all started back to camp. We had thought it would be easier going downhill, but we were so worn out we could hardly keep on our feet. We staggered along as if drunk. Hu, the well-trained ecologist, marched in front of us as if nothing were amiss. We would have given the world to sit down for a while and rest. Now and then Hu would glance back and note the sorry state we were in, but he never stopped. It was not that he was unsympathetic; he was simply afraid that if we didn't make it back before dusk, our friends at Camp 51 would worry about our safety and feel they had to come looking for us with flashlights.

A FIRESIDE CHAT WITH DR. SCHALLER

The log cabin was divided evenly into two spaces: One half served as a kitchen, and the other half as a combination dining room, meeting room, and common room. At the end of a hard day's work, everyone relaxed there, sitting by the fire and chatting over a hot meal. With us were Dr. George Schaller—the noted ecologist and director of Wildlife Conservation International of the New York Zoological Society, who was on assignment with the World Wildlife Fund—and his wife, Kay.

Mrs. Schaller was always ready to laugh and chat with anyone, but Dr. Schaller, like Hu Jinchu, was a man of action who rarely had much to say. As we were relaxing after dinner, I told him that we had seen the feces of a panda but, regrettably, not the panda itself. He said, "The first time I ever saw a panda in the open and not in a zoo was after I had been here two months. I can hardly describe my feelings."

I hastened to reply that we had come a long way with the same desire. I was hoping that he and Hu would understand our eagerness and create the necessary conditions for us to see the panda. Our sincerity must have moved them, for Schaller suggested that Hu take us the next day to locate a panda by radio receiver, and to my delight, Hu agreed.

The rest of our conversation was informal and lively, covering a wide range of topics—the giant panda's present condition and prospects for the future, wildlife protection and scientific research in general, the Wolong Nature Reserve and the captive pandas in Japan, Mexico, and the United States. Finally, we touched on the radio collars that have been placed around the necks of some giant pandas. I asked how this device helped in studying the panda's ecology.

Schaller told us that the collar's tiny radio transmitter—powered by a fingernail-size battery that lasts one and a half to two years—sends out signals that reveal the whereabouts of the panda, while the frequency of the signals indicates whether the panda is moving or resting. "It's as simple as that," Schaller explained, "but by monitoring and recording these signals over a long time

The Panda Research Center

The author (center) with George Schaller and Hu Jinchu at Camp 51

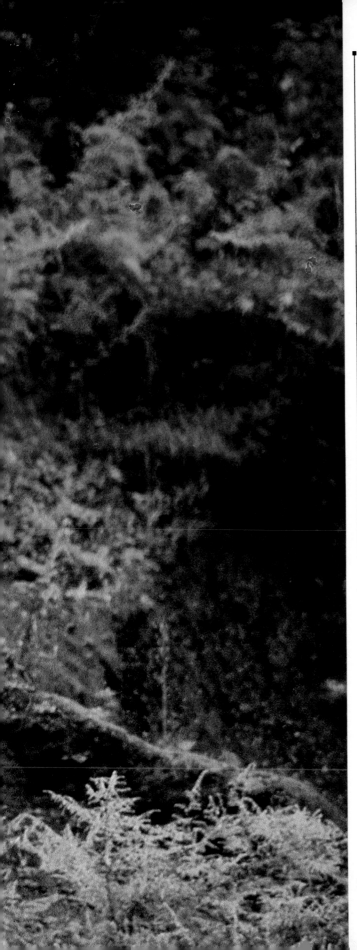

and analyzing the records, we can learn many, many things. We can determine the panda's general pattern of activity. For example, we have learned that the giant panda usually lives by itself, and while it does not stay in one fixed place, it keeps to a very limited routine of activity. It roves around and eats almost nonstop day and night, taking only short rests. From the change in the frequency of the signal during different seasons, we can also tell whether the panda is in heat, mating, and so forth. For the moment, only Zhen-Zhen, Long-Long, and Ning-Ning are wearing collars. If it were possible for more pandas to wear collars, we could expand our research into the structure of panda society."

I had been told that male pandas in zoos rarely got sexually excited or even cooperative with females. "Is it the same out here?" I asked Dr. Schaller.

Taking a walk in the wilderness

Hu Jinchu monitoring Zhen-Zhen, Ning-Ning, and Long-Long with a mini-radio receiver

He replied in two brief sentences, then burst out laughing. His wife also got into a laughing fit, burying her face in his shoulder. Our interpreter blushed and started laughing, too, but did not translate. Puzzled, we insisted that he tell us what Dr. Schaller had said. Finally the interpreter explained: "Dr. Schaller says that the male panda has a much stronger sexual urge than he has himself." Now the whole cabin was roaring with laughter. Although he was making a joke, Dr. Schaller spoke with authority, for he had been present during a complete session of lovemaking between Zhen-Zhen and her lover, and had even recorded how many times they coupled.

At our urging, he told us what had happened. About mid-April the signals from Zhen-Zhen's collar increased in frequency. She seemed restless and in heat. At the same time the cries of another giant panda could be heard nearby, so the scientists began round-the-clock field observation. Sure enough, a male panda was seen with Zhen-Zhen. Soon they were heard growling, grunting, snarling, panting—preparing to make love. But then another, smaller male panda arrived. The two males faced off against each other, but did not really get into a fight; each appeared to be trying to scare off the other with a lot of howling and growling. The smaller male was driven away several times but kept coming back, until finally, clearly disappointed at his inability to overpower his rival, he left for good. Once he was gone, the two pandas started their mating session in a bamboo thicket.

Watching this extraordinary scene, Schaller and his assistants did not sleep for twenty-four hours. Unfortunately, the thickness of the bamboo prevented them from taking photographs. Only once, as the two pandas rolled down the side of a trail, did Schaller manage to hide behind a big tree and shoot from a distance of less than seven feet. In a little over two hours the pair mated forty-eight times, and the male would have continued, but Zhen-Zhen grew weary. To get away from her persistent lover, she climbed a big tree. The male panda

had no alternative but to leave, sullenly; since then, there had been no sign of him.

ZHEN-ZHEN'S HOME

That night I slept badly. Lying in the tent, I listened to the sound of water endlessly dripping outside. It seemed to be raining and I worried that nothing would come of our plan to find a panda by radio. At daybreak Hu told me that what I had heard was not rain. A heavy fog had settled in, and the moisture had collected on the leaves and then trickled to the ground. Nevertheless, he said, the dense fog would make it difficult to track the panda today, and going through the forest we would get soaked to the skin. Seeing our obvious disappointment, he added, "We'll go see Zhen-Zhen. If she's out, we can even visit her nest."

We started off on a different path. Zhen-Zhen, Long-Long, and Ning-Ning were close neighbors, all living on one side or the other of the mountain ridge. Normally, an observer from Camp 51 climbed this path at least once a day. While Zhen-Zhen was in heat, mating, and giving birth to her cub, the scientists stayed in a tent high up on the mountain to monitor her movements every fifteen minutes, day and night. Along the path we saw the wooden cage in which Zhen-Zhen had been caught for collaring, and the scratches on the bark of trees where the two pandas had mated. I found myself wondering why we had to wait for Zhen-Zhen to leave before visiting her nest. Hu told us what had happened when he and Dr. Schaller had tried to pay a visit to Zhen-Zhen's cub.

After Zhen-Zhen gave birth, everyone was eager to find out whether she had had one or two cubs and whether they were male or female. But the scientists knew better than to go too soon. They were familiar with the way felines protect their young. If disturbed, the mother will move her young elsewhere or even kill

Pandas mating

them. Pandas are not cats, of course. Their nearest relatives appear to be the raccoons, although some experts classify them as aberrant bears. However, Hu and Schaller were afraid that Zhen-Zhen might react the same way a feline might, so they waited until her cub was two months old before going up the mountain.

Guided by the radio signals, they found Zhen-Zhen in less than twenty minutes. In the past she had always been quite friendly toward them, but this time she charged them with a menacing howl. Frightened, Hu turned and ran, but in his haste he went in the wrong direction, toward the panda's nest. Naturally this made

Zhen-Zhen even more furious. But now Hu drew on his experience. He ran as fast as he could up the hill. The giant panda, being fat and clumsy, was less agile going up the slope than going down, so Hu managed to remain out of her reach. Only after Hu had moved well away from her nest did Zhen-Zhen stop pursuing him. Schaller, who had been walking behind Hu, climbed a tree in fear. Although he was carrying all the photographic equipment, he forgot completely to take pictures of this perilous encounter. Nevertheless, there was one reward— they both heard the little cub squealing in its nest.

That was the last time they had disturbed Zhen-Zhen. As we climbed, Hu, still a little fearful, urged us in a low voice to speed up; we should by all means avoid a meeting with Zhen-Zhen.

When we reached the observation station known as 4X, at an altitude of 9,676 feet, Hu fetched a radio receiver and a portable aerial from the tent there. First we monitored Ning-Ning. Hu informed us: "The lazy creature is still asleep." He intensified the receiver's signal, so we could hear it, too. The frequency was slower than that of a human pulse. Then we turned to Long-Long's signal. The frequency was quite fast, indicating that Long-Long was either roaming about or looking for food. Lastly, we monitored Zhen-Zhen. Hu told us regretfully: "Zhen-Zhen does not welcome you. She is guarding her nest." We were very disappointed, but there was nothing we could do about it.

Liu was tired and decided to stay in the tent to rest while Hu and I climbed to observation station 6X, then to 11X. We had just left the tent at 11X when suddenly we heard a noise like a pig squealing.

"What is it?"

"Zhen-Zhen's cub."

I was overjoyed. It was the panda's cry! Thank you, little one, for saying hello to me. On behalf of all the people in the world who are concerned about you, I hope you grow up in good health!

Hu remarked, "Long-Long is down below, not far away. If the bamboo were not so wet, we'd have no trouble finding him."

By that time, however, I felt quite satisfied and did not want to ask the impossible, so we descended to where we had left Liu. While we were picnicking, we threw some biscuits to the squirrels, who, bushy tails held high, came scampering right to our feet to ask for more.

It was getting dark as we made our way back. A few hundred meters from Camp 51 we heard the snapping of branches, followed by what sounded like a birdcall. What was it? Again the same sharp snapping sound. "Perhaps the golden monkeys," Hu muttered. He immediately quickened his pace. After a few steps he pushed aside the brushwood and called excitedly, "Look, hurry!" I hastened after him, into the tall trees, shrubs, bamboos. My eyes blurred; I could see nothing.

Liu had sharper eyesight. "A golden monkey!" he exclaimed, delighted. "How beautiful! It's a big one and it's looking in our direction. There's another one . . . oh, quite a number of them!" The more he exclaimed, the more excited I became and the less I could see. Then the old monkey evidently noticed us and quickly led his protégés away. Soon all the golden monkeys had disappeared into the forest.

Seeing my disappointment, Hu consoled me, saying, "This may have been just the vanguard, and the main horde will be coming." We concentrated all our attention on looking for them until we arrived at Camp 51, but we saw no more golden monkeys. The main horde had passed, we were told, some ten minutes before.

FOUR QUESTIONS THAT NEED TO BE ANSWERED

I had gone to the Giant Panda Research Center with four questions in mind, four questions that everyone who loves pandas has been concerned about:

Camp 51, the Panda Research Center's observation post hidden in the woods

Coming down from the mountains in search of bamboo shoots

How many giant pandas are left?

Is the panda population increasing or decreasing?

What have we done so far to protect the giant panda?

What more can we do to ensure the survival of the giant panda?

Earlier, in Nanchong, I had attended a symposium on the giant panda which brought together scientists and specialists from research institutes, universities and colleges, zoos, and nature reserves. I listened to scientific reports and discussions, and exchanged views with experts on the physiology, biochemistry, diseases, and ecology of the giant panda and on the protective measures already being taken. Now, at the Research Center in Wolong, I had direct contact with both Chinese and foreign investigators who were studying the giant panda. Although I have not yet found definitive answers to all my questions, I have learned much.

How many giant pandas are left?

Two figures are needed to answer this question. The first is verifiable; the second is at best a "guesstimate."

We can count the number of pandas in zoos and breeding farms. Before the founding of the People's Republic of China in 1949, more than twenty foreign expeditions had come to China to catch pandas. They took away sixteen live pandas (two of which died en route to their new homes) and eighteen skins. Four of these captive pandas were still alive in 1949 but died soon after. On various occasions since then, the Chinese government has presented to foreign countries another twenty-three pandas, some of which have died. Meanwhile, pandas have been bred in several countries, leaving about fifteen giant pandas outside China. In China more than eighty pandas are kept in over thirty zoos (including the Shanghai Circus), and the breeding farms in the nature reserves have ten pandas altogether. So the giant pandas in captivity add up to just over a hundred.

Since the giant panda hides in high mountains and deep valleys, it is very difficult to make an accurate count of the animals in the wild. Several counts have been taken over the past ten years with several different methods, but it has proved impossible to come up with a figure everyone can accept. Most experts go along with a rough estimate of about a thousand giant pandas in the world, both in captivity and in the wild.

Is the panda population increasing or decreasing?

It seems clear that even if all killing and capturing of giant pandas were to stop, the animal would still be on the verge of extinction.

Several trends indicate the danger. People living near panda habitats report seeing fewer pandas than in the past. In some areas where there was once a substantial population, there are only a few pandas today. In other places there are none. Records kept at Mount Emei in the first half of this century state, "Pandas abide in the forests that lie above the Wooden Temple." As late as 1948 the *Southeast Daily* reported the capture of a

Resting in the bamboo forest

giant panda on Mount Emei. Today, no pandas can be found there. Many historical records of earlier times mention giant pandas in Yunnan, Fujian, Guizhou, and Hubei provinces. An analysis of available fossil material suggests that during the Pleistocene epoch the giant panda was distributed widely in neighboring countries of South Asia, as well as in south, central, and north China as far as the region of Beijing and Zhoukoudian (near Beijing) where the skull of Peking man was found in 1927.

Surveyors, too, report finding fewer feces, nests, and traces of food indicating the presence of giant pandas. Once, panda feces could be collected by the basketful, but today this is rare.

The great majority of giant pandas seen in the wild are adults; very few cubs have been sighted. In a six-month survey recently carried out by the staff of the Fuping Nature Reserve, only two of the sixteen giant pandas observed were cubs (unlike golden monkeys, which were typically seen with a number of young).

The reproduction rate of the giant panda is lower than the death rate. We have a twenty-year history of breeding pandas in China, yet so far only ten pandas have been bred in captivity, while several times that number have died. If a 1978 survey carried out at Choushuigou in the Wolong Nature Reserve is any indication, the reproduction rate of giant pandas in the wild is also very low. That year only eight of twenty-one adult pandas were in heat and mated, and only one nest with a newborn panda was discovered.

The reasons for the decline of the giant-panda population fall into two categories: biological and environmental.

First, the biological. In evolutionary terms, the giant panda is a remnant species. Just as all living creatures go through three different phases—birth, development, and decline—so has the panda species. The giant panda has now entered its decline. It lacks agility, has trouble fending off enemies, persists in nonadaptive eating habits, and maintains a low fertility rate. Originally the giant panda was a carnivore. It now subsists mainly on a monotonous diet of bamboo, not because it cannot eat meat but because, with its poor eyesight and lack of speed, it is unable to hunt prey. As a matter of fact, the giant panda is quite fond of picking at carcasses left by other carnivorous animals. One can capture a giant panda by luring it to a cage baited with cooked meat on the bone.

The giant panda is a solitary creature and does not like to roam far. Except for brief journeys straight up or down a mountain once or twice a year when the bamboo sprouts, it usually keeps to a range of about two square kilometers (less than five hundred acres). In its isolation (which is further reinforced by human harassment), inbreeding has clearly led to genetic defects. Difficulties in mating, due at least in part to the unusual structure of the panda's sexual organs, the difficulty females have in conceiving and giving birth, the low survival rate among cubs—all these factors no doubt contribute to the decline of the panda population. Similar problems can be seen among captive pandas. For example, of the five male giant pandas in the Chengdu

Zoo, only one showed an inclination to mate, but none of the females was in heat at the time.

The environmental reasons for the decline of the giant panda are even easier to enumerate.

THE DAMAGE CAUSED BY MAN. The cutting down of forests, cultivation of land, pasturing of cattle, dynamiting of mountains to construct roads—all these activities have severely constricted the panda's habitat. Over the centuries this habitat shrank from vast regions to one long strip of land, which shrank again to scattered localities, until today it is limited to a few isolated places, such as the Min Mountains, Qionglai Mountains, Greater and Lesser Xiang Mountains, Greater and Lesser Liang Mountains, and the southern slopes of the Qinling Mountains. While most of the shrinkage was caused indirectly by the expansion of human economic activities, men must also be blamed for their indiscriminate hunting and capturing of the giant panda.

SECOND, NATURAL DISASTERS. The arrow bamboo, which is the giant panda's favorite food, flowers and withers in regular cycles. In 1975, when wide stretches of bamboo in Wen County, Gansu Province, and in Pingwu and Nanping counties, Sichuan Province, flowered and withered away, great numbers of pandas starved to death. Afterward, 138 panda carcasses were discovered. Since 1983 many areas of bamboo have gone through a similar cycle, but because the phenomenon caught the world's attention, total disaster was avoided. As the result of urgent rescue efforts, only twelve pandas died.

THIRD, NATURAL ENEMIES, MAINLY THE LEOPARD, ASIATIC WILD DOG, AND BROWN BEAR. There are records of these animals harming pandas in Tianquan, Qingchuan, Wenchuan, and Baoxing coun-

A panda drinking at a stream

32

ties. Two giant pandas were devoured by leopards at the Wolong Nature Reserve in 1979 and another one in 1981. The pandas attacked by these beasts are usually young animals that have just left their mothers. In 1983, Zhen-Zhen's cub also disappeared—perhaps eaten by natural enemies.

FOURTH, DISEASE, PARTICULARLY ASCARIASIS (ROUNDWORM DISEASE). As many as 60 to 70 percent of all giant pandas suffer from this disease, which, even when it is not fatal, seriously retards growth and reproduction.

So even if the panda is not hunted, it may still, for all these reasons, be disappearing from the world stage.

What have we done so far to protect the giant panda?
One figure tells the story. If we add up all the people directly concerned with the giant panda, people who work in the giant-panda reserves, all those in charge of pandas in zoos, and all those working in research institutes and university and college departments, the total is approximately a thousand—which is equal to the estimated population of giant pandas in the world. If we include people who are indirectly involved with the welfare of the giant panda, the number is even larger.

China is by no means the only country concerned about the giant panda. In fact, concern for the survival of the species seems especially intense outside China, perhaps because pandas are so rare there. The World Wildlife Fund collaborated with Chinese authorities in establishing the Research Center for the Conservation of the Giant Panda at Wolong. Only a few countries have successfully bred pandas. The London Zoo's giant panda was flown across the ocean to meet his bride in the United States. Unfortunately, the pair was ill-matched and spent an unhappy (and unfruitful) honeymoon, after which the marriage broke up. In the first-class panda home that the West Berlin Zoo built, the panda sleeps on a "bed" that is actually a huge scale, so that the animal's weight can be recorded daily. The panda's

Playing a game after a full meal

food is prepared in a special kitchen; bamboo is flown in from France by special plane. In London the giant-panda pavilion is also a fully equipped research institute. Drawing on experience acquired in breeding other rare animals, British scientists are carrying out artificial insemination by introducing semen directly into the female panda's ovaries.

In China itself, much has been done in many areas. Thirteen nature reserves, covering more than 636,000 hectares (almost 2,500 square miles), have been established mainly for the conservation of the giant panda. Only when this step was taken to preserve the giant panda's natural habitat was it possible to proceed with other measures. Through wide publicity over the years, everyone has been made familiar with the need to protect the panda, and the capture or killing of giant pandas has been virtually eliminated—a major achievement considering that harmful attacks on other rare animals still occur all too frequently.

In addition, after many years of scientific investigation we now have a basic understanding of the giant panda's ecology—its habitat, its food resources, its behavior (including its reproductive habits), the social structure of its population, and the effect on the giant panda of man's activities. In recent years, advanced research techniques, such as tracing the panda's movements by radio, have provided new information vital for improving protection measures.

Progress has also been made in breeding giant pandas in captivity. Experience has brought knowledge about the oestrous period of the female panda, about how to collect semen and how to freeze it, about methods of artificial insemination, and about the rearing of cubs. Since 1963 the zoos in Beijing, Chengdu, Shanghai, Kunming, and Hangzhou have successfully bred twenty giant pandas through natural mating and eight others through artificial insemination.

All this proves that man has the means to protect the panda. Which brings us to our last question.

What more can we do to ensure the survival of the giant panda?

The answer is: We have only begun to fight the decline of the giant panda, and a great deal of organizational and scientific work still has to be done. To carry out all the tasks that remain, we will have to mobilize even greater forces than before. Hu Jinchu stressed the magnitude of the challenge by saying: "Only when there is hope of modernizing China can there be hope for conservation of the giant panda." He did not speak

unreasonably, as we can see by looking at some of the tasks ahead.

Certainly the system of nature reserves has to be expanded and perfected to guarantee preservation of the panda's habitat. In the reserves as they are now, the pandas live in a state of somewhat unnatural isolation. Moreover, some of the nature reserves exist in name only; man is still engaged in economic activities that harass the giant panda. In order to create the most favorable environmental conditions for the survival and increase of the panda, it will be necessary to learn more about such factors as protective cover, food and water resources, climate, natural enemies, disease, and competitors. Particular attention should be paid to the flowering and withering of the bamboo. The growth cycle of bamboo and its relation to climate, soil, moisture, and other factors should be studied. Different varieties of bamboo should be planted where the panda lives, so as to vary the flowering season; alternatively, a single variety could be planted at different times to create staggered growth cycles.

To tempt giant pandas to expand their range of activity, and to give them more opportunities to meet and mate, we might consider planting corridors of bamboo within the nature reserves and between different reserves. We might also try to control the numbers of predators that threaten the panda, provided this could be done without disturbing the ecological balance.

Second, the many agencies now employed in the conservation, study, breeding, and exhibition of the giant panda are not sufficiently integrated. Even within a single department, communication is sometimes minimal; much work is wastefully duplicated because colleagues do not exchange ideas or share experiences. Only when all departments cooperate in true multidisciplinary research, and the work is coordinated on a national scale, will breakthroughs in some major problems be possible.

Third, artificial breeding of the panda must be advanced to make up for inadequate natural breeding. If

Climbing a tree

pandas in captivity can exchange genes with those in the wild, inbreeding can be reduced and conditions can be created for the rejuvenation of the panda population. However, some problems in artificial breeding have not yet been solved. For example, why do male pandas in captivity have so little sex drive? Has this to do with their diet, environment, or something else? Can we find an efficient method of monitoring the oestrous period of the female panda so as to increase the rate of success in artificial insemination? At present the survival rate of panda cubs is very low. Only ten of the twenty-eight cubs bred artificially have survived. We need to improve equipment and methods for artificial nursing of baby pandas. If these problems are solved, it may be possible to increase several fold the success rate of artificial breeding of the giant panda.

In addition, breakthroughs achieved with the giant panda may open up new prospects for conserving other rare animals.

As my visit to the Wolong Nature Reserve drew to an end, I realized that, apart from not having seen Zhen-Zhen, all the goals of my journey had been achieved. When I expressed my gratitude to the experts, Chinese and foreign, who had been my hosts, they agreed that I had been fortunate: "In a few days you have seen what normally takes a much longer time to see." As for what I had missed, they assured me: "You are welcome to return to the Giant Panda Research Center, and try again."

SAVING THE PANDAS

In May 1983 terrible news came from the panda's homeland: The bamboo plants, the chief food of the giant panda, were beginning to flower and wither. Research has shown that bamboo plants flower only at long intervals. Arrow bamboo, for example, flowers every fifty or sixty years, and the new bamboo plants need ten years or longer to mature. An adult panda usually eats thirty-three pounds of bamboo stems or eighty-eight pounds of bamboo shoots a day, so this flowering and withering can have serious consequences. People remembered the disaster of 1975, when 138 pandas starved to death because of the bamboo's flowering.

This time, the damage done to the mainstay of the panda's diet appeared to be even more severe, and the area affected even larger, than in 1975. It would not be easy to rescue all the pandas threatened by starvation in Sichuan, Shaanxi, and Gansu provinces and in the other habitats. In response to the news, the Chinese government organized an emergency task force headed by Dong Zhiyong, Vice-Minister of Forestry and vice-president of the China Wildlife Preservation Association. The sum of 2.6 million yuan ($650,000 US) was appropriated, and local governments, nature reserves, and panda research centers all joined enthusiastically in the rescue effort. The World Wildlife Fund issued a special bulletin. Scientists, politicians, artists, and thousands of students in China and abroad took part in activities to raise money to help the pandas.

In a very short time more than fifty special patrols were dispatched to the 8,000–10,000-foot mountains and dense forests of the panda's homeland. Their mission: investigate the losses caused by the disaster, enforce hunting regulations, and protect surviving bamboo plants from fire. In severely hit areas three methods were adopted to save the weakened pandas. First, a large quantity of meat was scattered

A starving panda is carried down the mountain.

along paths to lure the pandas down from the mountains. Second, pandas that could not be lured down were trapped, carried down the mountains in cages, and fed until they recovered. (In Sichuan Province more than thirty dying pandas were saved by this method in six months.) Third, feeding posts were set up for the few strong, healthy pandas.

The rescue operation was a heartening success; despite the greater severity of the problem, the death rate in 1983 was only one tenth of that suffered in the 1975 disaster. But statistics tell only part of the story of the personal concern and dedication that helped save so many pandas. In Lushan County a peasant named Gao Yuelun went up a mountain with a goat and a dog to till some land. Suddenly a hungry panda appeared and sprang at the goat. To keep from frightening the panda, Gao stopped the dog from barking and hid himself and the dog until the panda had finished eating the goat. In Baoxing County a woman who saw a panda being swept away in a turbulent river jumped into the cold water and rescued it. Then she warmed it, gave it some water, and fed it bamboo plants, before taking it to a panda feeding station. Now this panda is faring very well.

A panda being fed at Camp 51

FIVE MORE CRESTED IBISES HAVE TAKEN WING

Five more crested ibises *(Nipponia nippon)* have taken wing!

This is inspiring news, since it means that the number of crested ibises in the world has increased by 25 percent. It indicates progress in the struggle to bring this species—among the world's most endangered—back from the brink of extinction.

I was fortunate to be one of the first observers of the newly airborne creatures. When I arrived in Yang County, Shaanxi Province, two of the ibis nestlings were still in the nest waiting to be fed, two were perched on branches flapping their wings, eager to fly like their parents, while the fifth had already followed its parents into the field to look for food. By the time I left Yang County, all had left the nest and moved to secondary feeding areas or places farther off. Their faces and feet had not yet turned scarlet and their feathers looked whiter than those of adult birds, but by late autumn they would look so much like their parents that no one would be able to tell them apart.

THE EXCITEMENT OF TAKING PICTURES

Crested Ibis Group No. 1 is located in the Qinling Range Preservation Station at Yaojiagou, the center of activity for ibis preservation. Yaojiagou is thirty-seven miles from the county seat and three miles from the end of the bus route at the foot of the mountain. From there one must proceed on foot along a mountain road up the southern slope of the Qinling Range. Yaojiagou itself is midway up the mountain at an elevation of 4,451 feet above sea level at latitude 33°32' north and longitude 107°37' east, a transitional area between the northern subtropics and the temperate zone. It consists of a long, narrow ravine inhabited by seven families working twenty-odd *mu* (over three acres) of rice paddies. Advanced agricultural techniques have not been introduced into this out-of-the-

way place, and people seldom use chemical fertilizers and pesticides. This circumstance, together with the cultivation of some winter paddies, provides suitable living conditions for the ibises.

In order to survive, crested ibises must have access to tall trees near paddies, where they can fish for food, in a remote location, where they are relatively safe from their natural enemies. The key to their survival in Yaojiagou is a group of fifteen old oriental oak trees *(Quercus variabilis)* on the north slope. This is where the ibises have made their nests. It is extremely rare now in any region to find such a group of old trees growing right beside a village. The trees have remained untouched because they are growing in a graveyard, which the villagers have refrained from disturbing. According to the tablets there, the graves date from 1834, so the oriental oak trees are at least 150 years old. Without these venerable trees, there would be no place for the ibises to live.

Because Yaojiagou provides all the right conditions, it has become a fairly stable breeding ground for ibises. Elsewhere in Yang County we found many places where ibises had once nested but where, for various reasons, the nestlings had not been able to survive. In Yaojiagou ibises have hatched every year since 1981. So far, ten have survived—half the world's total of crested ibises.

When I first arrived in Yaojiagou, on June 2, 1984, I saw two ibises looking for fish and other aquatic creatures in the paddies. I was struck by the beauty of their long bills, shaggy crests, scarlet faces, and snow-white feathers. Excited to find before my eyes a bird I had long hoped to see, I pulled out my camera and began to approach them.

My companion warned, "They won't let you near." When I asked about the farmers plowing the fields right beside them, he replied that the birds had come to know and accept the local people, but a stranger would immediately put them on the alert.

A baby bird has grown as big as his parents.

Soaring through the sky

Just as he had predicted, when I came within about two hundred yards of the ibises, they took off, flapping their large wings. The sun's golden light illuminated their snow-white feathers as they swept past the dark-green rice seedlings and over the verdant hills. No wonder they have been called the celestials of Qinling!

After lunch we set off immediately for their living area. We tramped through the bushes looking for a good place to take pictures. In tree number 5, on a branch about fifty-five feet from the ground, was a nest with two chicks inside; a third chick stood on a branch six feet away.

They must have seen us but they did not budge. Perhaps they had grown used to having strangers stand under their nest watching them. Occasionally they changed positions or stretched their wings as if to show that they did not care what we did with our cameras.

It was on this day that I first experienced the thrill of nature photography. Just to see the ibises was exciting, but it was even more exciting to know that my camera was focused on three of only twenty ibises left in the world—and these were not the three old caged ibises in Japan or the one in the Beijing Zoo, but free birds in the wild.

I took one picture after another, but Lao Wu, who stood beside me, seldom pressed the shutter. He had taken pictures of the crested ibis many times and was more patient. He whispered to me: "Let's wait for the old ibis to return. Its red cheeks make it even more attractive."

We both waited then, our cameras at the ready.

It is easy to hold a camera in position for a short while, but as the minutes passed, our arms began to ache; yet neither of us dared relax for fear of missing the moment when the old ibis flew back to the nest. An employee of the ibis preservation station had told me that a parent bird usually stayed out for an hour hunting for food, but our wait seemed much longer than that. Perhaps the parent bird had seen two strangers under the nest and dared not come back.

Parent birds returning to the nest

My eyes grew tired and my hands began to shake from holding the camera in readiness for so long. From time to time I let my arms down to rest them, but only for a moment. My attention was concentrated to the highest degree. I began to appreciate how hard it was to take a valuable picture.

At last the parent bird could no longer restrain its instinct to feed and protect its babies, and it returned.

First, a low sound of flight emerged from the forest, then a big pink ibis flew into the range of our lenses. The clicks of two cameras were heard, one after the other. For me, it was a soul-stirring, unforgettable moment. It has been said that all artistic creation requires emotional excitement, and photography is perhaps the most impulsive art. The photographer must be ready at any moment to capture a scene that arouses his spirit.

Teaching the children to fly

The nestlings were impatient as the parent reached them. Some were crying or flapping their wings. A strong young ibis plunged its long bill into the parent bird's mouth and pulled out some half-digested food. The parent fed the babies one by one, emptying its throat of food, then left the nest again to look for more. All this took but a few moments. There was no time to think about artistic composition. My mind was fully occupied with taking advantage of every second to capture what I saw on film.

DIARY OF A FAMILY

The year 1984 witnessed a breakthrough in efforts to preserve the crested ibis. Peasants in Sanchahe reported finding the nest of a pair of crested ibises. From information given us by the local people and from traces of old nests, we concluded that Sanchahe might be a stable breeding place for the crested ibis.

When I arrived in Sanchahe, located in an even more remote area than Yaojiagou, the villagers were curious about me and eagerly asked me questions. They had never met anyone from Beijing. An employee of the preservation station told me I was the first visitor from the capital to pay a call on the crested ibis.

The surroundings of Sanchahe are similar to Yaojiagou's, providing a suitable environment for the crested ibis. Near the village, which is 3,600 feet above sea level, a group of tall oriental oak trees grow in an old graveyard on a hill. According to the gravestone inscriptions, these trees are even older than the trees in Yaojiagou. There was a nest in one of the trees. A family named Luo lived nearby and worked a large paddy. To the west were more families and a large area of paddies, with other families and paddies scattered in a ravine lower down. Altogether, 39 families (182 people) and 122 *mu* (20 acres) of paddies made up this village.

Unfortunately a steady rain started the day after I arrived. The ravines quickly filled with water and the roads turned to mud. I had no way to get down the mountain, nor could the jeep come for me. But these

Sanchahe, a typical habitat of the crested ibis, with tall trees, a paddy field

clouds, too, had a silver lining, for they gave me a good chance to study the crested ibis. Every day I went out barefoot to observe the birds, then I went from house to house, visiting the local people. I also had an opportunity to talk to the employees of the observation station and to read through their "Ibis Observation Record." Although many of the notations are straightforward and rather dry, one series of entries records in fascinating detail how the crested ibis raises its young.

April 27, 1984

Yesterday we received a telephone call informing us that crested ibises had been discovered in Sanchahe. We set off immediately from Yaojiagou, climbing over ridges for more than forty kilometers [twenty-five miles] on a mountain road and arriving here yesterday morning.

Today we saw a crested ibis in the paddy next to the home of the Luo family. But where was the nest? Our experience told us that it must be in one of the tall trees in the graveyard. At 10:10 A.M. we found a nest on a branch of a *Quercus variabilis* tree near the paddy. Its position, height, materials, and structure were all more or less the same as in Yaojiagou. We also saw the heads of crested ibises

Leaving the nest and looking for food on their own.

moving in the nest and could tell that they were over ten days old, but we couldn't determine the number of ibises in the nest because the tree branches and parent bird blocked our view from the opposite side of the hill.

April 29

Today we were able to see clearly three nestlings. We took some pictures and numbered the thirty-seven *Quercus variabilis* trees. One of them is dead and another has a ring cut out of it about waist height. Luckily it was not cut down and remains alive today. Trunks of other large trees were lying on the ground. It looks as if we were just in time. If we had come later, the trees would all have been cut down.

April 30

We arrived beneath the nest tree at 7:20 this morning. The parent birds had gone out to look for food. Ten minutes later, one ibis flew back. It gave the nestlings ten feedings altogether. The other parent came back at 10:43. It gave eleven feedings. Perhaps they had noticed us or perhaps it was for some other reason, but after 10:51 the two parent birds began to take turns watching the nest. One did not leave the nest until the other returned.

At noon neither left the nest. One parent preened one of the nestlings while the other fixed up the nest. The ibis nest is simple, and ibises usually expand and strengthen it during the hatching and brooding periods.

May 4

As the three nestlings fight over their food, it becomes clearer and clearer which is strongest and which weakest. Today we saw them pecking at each other. The strongest was taking food from the parent bird's bill while the other two stood aside with heads lowered. The second got its turn to be fed only when the strongest was completely full or was forced to stop by the parent bird. The smallest was so weak and timid that it often got nothing to eat. All it could do was hang its head in weariness and hunger.

May 5

As the nestlings' food requirement has increased, the parents have had to go out searching more often. Today we observed from 5:35 in the morning until 19:50 in the evening. The two parents went out thirteen times each to look for food and ten times to gather nest material.

This was not a record. An ibis we observed in Yaojiagou made seventeen trips a day in search of

A. Chicks waiting for the return of their mother

B. Here she comes

C. Feeding the young

food. It took back an average of six loaches [carplike fish] each time, or 102 loaches a day. The average weight of each loach was 9.8 grams, or 1,097.6 grams in all. During the feeding period the parent birds are so busy that they lose weight, while the nestlings grow bigger day by day.

May 9

Someone came to tell us that Wang Qingbao's dog had been chasing a crested ibis and had nearly caught it. We went to Wang's home and explained to him the importance of protecting the crested ibis. We asked him to sell the dog, offering to pay for it. He promised to tie the dog and keep it under control.

Others have told us that last year an eagle wounded one crested ibis and flew off with another one. Can this be possible? We need to investigate this more thoroughly. On the whole, the relationship between the crested ibis and other animals is still a considerable mystery and a topic worth researching.

May 13

At 9:00 this morning the three nestlings were stirring in their nest as they waited for food. It was 9:30 before one of the parents flew back. It fed one baby, then flew away again. At 10:10 the other parent came. It also fed one baby and left. It was clear there was a food crisis. The small size of the paddy and the low temperatures are unfavorable for the growth of aquatic creatures such as loaches, other fish, and river snails. No matter how hard the parent birds tried, they had difficulty finding enough food to meet the needs of the three almost-grown nestlings. The scramble for food among the three became fiercer and fiercer. If we hadn't scattered food ourselves, the weakest would have starved. It was the same in Yaojiagou and at the Beijing Zoo. At present a method of food distribution has been devised in Yaojiagou, but we have no way to do the same here, because the high mountains and long distance from town make it difficult to bring food in.

May 15

At 9:30 A.M. two of the young were playing on branches three meters [about ten feet] from their nest while the other one was still lying in the nest, too weak to get up. The strongest one is getting stronger while the weakest is getting weaker. I am really worried that the weak bird may not survive.

The parents have treated their young fairly. At 10:15 a parent returned. It began to feed the weak bird in the nest, but then the other two came back, pecked the weak bird aside and started snatching the food out of the parent's bill. At 3:00 P.M. the two birds were again playing merrily on a branch, but the poor weak bird was back in the nest, miserable and hungry.

May 16

At 10:00 in the morning the parents were out, the two stronger birds were playing near the nest, and the weak bird was lying in the nest.

It rained heavily today. At 11:00 we gave up, finding it impossible to observe.

It stopped raining at 5:00 P.M. We arrived at the nest tree at 5:40. A parent was perched on a branch about five meters [sixteen feet] from the nest. Two young were on a branch near the nest, but to our surprise the weak bird had disappeared. Where was it? Had it been carried off by an enemy or did it fall from the nest?

We looked under the tree. Within minutes we found it dead in a spot about three meters from the nest tree. Its tail was pointing downhill and its head was tucked under its body, with one wing spread out. The body was not yet completely cold and we found no wounds. When we touched its

stomach, we could tell there was no food at all in it. We were quite upset and wanted to report immediately to the preservation station, but the regular time for radio communication was not until 7:30 the next morning. We waited impatiently.

Hunger was the cause of death. Perhaps it had been scrambling for food, or the strong winds and heavy rain may have blown it from the nest. But why had it died? The bird that fell from its nest in Yaojiagou in 1981 was no bigger than this one. It fell three times without being killed. Were this bird's wings wet or did it bump into something? Or was it already on the point of death?

May 17

At 5:50 this morning the two young were running from branch to branch, flapping their wings, as if they cared nothing about the death of their brother. But this was not the case with the parents. As one parent flew back from a nearby cornfield and landed on a branch by the nest, the two rushed to it for food, but the parent paid no attention to them, just stood there with a dull look in its eyes as if it were still thinking of the terrible incident that occurred yesterday. A few moments later the other parent came back. It had not brought back any food for the young birds either.

The first parent flew toward the lower ravine, while the other gave three low cries, then landed in tree number 23. It cried twice more, as if it were calling its poor dead baby back. Our hearts were touched by this moving scene and the sound of their sad, shrill cries.

Later we saw the two parents looking for food in the paddy in front of Luo's house. We observed them carefully through binoculars. They were acting queerly, moving about slowly and without

A beautiful celestial

animation. Ten minutes later they were still walking back and forth aimlessly, having caught nothing.

After hearing our report, the people in the preservation station at once sent ten kilograms [twenty-two pounds] of loaches and threw them into the paddies near the nest at 7:00 this evening.

May 18

At 6:00 A.M. we observed that the two young were about five meters from the nest. One was trying its best to fly from one twig to another, and its first try was successful. It was quite satisfied with itself and continued flying back and forth between branches, gradually becoming braver and more confident.

The other one grew envious. It spread its wings and flapped them, but its feet still clung tight to the branch.

At 6:00 P.M. the first one wanted to fly farther. It reached tree number 8 without stopping—a rather long distance because the bird's wings are still not very strong, but it made it. Encouraged after a short rest, it flew over to tree number 1 and did not return to the nest until 7:00 in the evening.

May 19

The two young were perched on tree number 23.

At 12:08, 12:40, and 3:00 in the afternoon, the parents returned to feed their young. This showed that the situation had improved after we cast the loaches into the paddies.

At 3:30 in the afternoon the two young flew back to their nest, chirping proudly.

May 20

At 2:20 this afternoon one of the young set off from tree number 23, circled around tree number 1, then flew to the paddies. This was the first time

Flying practice

it had left the forest and flown to the open field. It dared not stay long in the field, however. It headed right back to tree number 23, and at 2:33 it flew back to the nest tree.

May 21

At 5:25 A.M. parents and young were all in the nest tree. At 5:44 they all went to the paddies, where the two young learned to catch fish. At 6:00 the parents flew to the lower ravine, while the two young returned to the nest tree. They played in the forest, flying from tree to tree and sometimes landing in the paddies alongside the forest.

May 22

At 9:00 this morning the parents took their young to the paddy in front of the Luo house to look for food. The two young had a hard time finding food and went crying to their parents for help, but the parents refused to feed them. They seemed to be saying: "Children, you are grown up now. You must do it yourselves."

The parents were very strict with their young but also very loving. At 5:03 P.M. the parents finally fed each bird once, so that they would not go hungry.

May 23

At 8:15 this morning one parent was in tree 23 and the other in tree 22. The two young joined the parent in tree 22. They did not know that the branch they landed on was dead and could not bear the weight of three birds. It broke with a crack. The frightened parent flew back and/forth, crying loudly. The two young wheeled through the air; then one landed on the nest tree and the other on tree 18. If this had happened five days earlier, they might have met the same fate as their lost sibling, but now their wings were strong enough to cope with any such emergencies. The frightened parent landed in tree 23. The other parent went over to it and, with gestures like those used during mating, calmed it down.

May 24

This morning at 10:10 three ibises were calling, swatting at one another, and chasing one another on tree 25.

How could such a fight have developed within the family? We took a closer look and found a strange bird among them.

Crested ibises are very territorial about their nests. Mainly because of the strict requirements for nest locations and the limited supply of food, especially during the breeding period, no other ibises may visit the nest. Crows and magpies can share the forests, even though they may invade the nests or take away building materials, because they do not compete for the same food.

The quarrel lasted an hour and a half, the sounds echoing through the valley; then the stranger must have felt it was in the wrong, or perhaps it was the weaker party, because at last it flew away toward the lower ravine and peace returned to this one.

June 3

After the young leave the nest, the family seldom goes back to it or uses it again, even during the breeding cycle. The ibises often land on the nest tree but do not go to the nest itself.

This morning in the fields the young birds again asked their parents for food, but they were refused. At 5:50 in the afternoon on tree number 4 they tried again but were again refused.

Landing among the rice seedlings

June 11

Early this morning we saw four birds in the paddy in front of the Luo house, but by 9:00 A.M. they had disappeared. We waited until evening, but they still did not come back.

Our experience told us that a breeding cycle was over and our ibises had flown off to new locations.

Good—bye, crested ibises. See you in the autumn.

WORN-OUT IRON SHOES

In 1979 the Chinese Academy of Sciences was assigned the job of looking for the crested ibis, a bird native to Asia and known as "the gem of the East." Classified as an internationally protected bird at the twelfth session of the World Conference for the Protection of Birds in 1960, the crested ibis has become extinct in the Soviet Union and Korea, while in Japan there are only a few left, all too old to breed. The only hope for rescuing the crested ibis rests with China.

The crested ibis is sometimes referred to as an egret, but it is a species of ibis. It was once widely distributed throughout China, as far north as Xingkai Lake, east to Fujian and Taiwan provinces, west to the Tianshui region of Gansu Province, and as far south as Hainan Island, but it was mainly found in the North, the Northeast, and around the Qinling Mountain. During the 1930's it was seen in fourteen provinces, but by the 1960's it could be found only in Yang County, Zhouzhi, and Xilan in Shaanxi Province. After that it disappeared without a trace.

Liu Yinzeng of the Beijing Institute of Zoology bravely took on the task of looking for the crested ibis, lost for twenty years. He studied the seventeen available specimens, consulted Chinese and foreign data, and analyzed the exploration routes of previous researchers. Then he set off with a map, a camera, and some research materials.

He traveled over mountains and waded across rivers. In three years he traversed half of China, covering more than thirteen provinces and about thirty thousand miles, but he did not find a single crested ibis or even a suitable environment for one. He did learn, however, that the most important reason for the apparent extinction of the crested ibis was the widespread and severe damage to its environment. He discovered that nearly all tall trees near villages had been cut down. Irrigated winter paddies no longer existed under the new crop system. Pesticides, chemical fertilizers, and waste water from factories had gravely polluted large areas of farmland and sources of water. In addition, the crested ibis usually lived in farming areas, where its large body and colorful feathers made it an easy target for hunters. The crested ibis also has many natural enemies, including crows, birds of prey, and yellow weasels, which often invade its nest, harm its eggs, and injure its young; its natural mortality is high. But damage to the environment was clearly the most important factor.

Liu Yinzeng also uncovered two important clues during his three years of exploration and investigation. First, he learned from a fisherman that ibises were living in Yang County, Shaanxi Province. Second, a hunter in Hui County, Gansu Province, gave him three feathers from an ibis killed only two or three years earlier.

When he returned to the Institute of Zoology, Liu made a detailed report. Administrators and specialists supported his request to continue the search, which would concentrate on Yang and Hui counties and a few other spots. They also provided him with a cross-country vehicle and increased his funding.

In 1981, Liu Yinzeng returned to Yang County for the third time. His research had indicated that crested ibises live at the foot of mountains; they cannot live at high elevations. After searching almost every part of Yang County with the proper elevation, Liu had still found no trace of the ibis. Just when he was about to move his search to Gansu Province, a peasant who had seen his slides told him that he had seen a "red crane." *Red crane* is the local name for the ibis, because its face and feet are red, and its wings appear red during flight. Liu Yinzeng was interested in the news, but he didn't fully believe it. He knew that there were a lot of egrets and herons in the area, and that the local people usually could not distinguish cranes and egrets from ibises. He took out a picture of the ibis and asked the peasant to look at the bird carefully and then report back. Two days later the peasant returned. He entered the room shouting loudly, "It's the right one! It looks exactly like the one in the picture."

They drove into the hills together. When the road became impassable, they got out of the vehicle and walked more than ten *li* (over three miles) until they reached Jinjiahe, 984 feet above sea level. There they found a nest bigger than an egret's and simpler than a magpie's—perhaps an ibis nest after all. Encouraged,

they spent another two days climbing in the mountains and hills. They were returning to Jinjiahe when, at three in the afternoon on May 21, they suddenly saw an ibis flying over them from east to west. No doubt about it—it was a crested ibis!

I asked Liu Yinzeng to describe how he felt at that moment. He said, "I'm not sure how excited I was. I just found myself saying, 'Ibis, what made you come to such a high mountain to live?' "

It was not that the research records had deceived him or that the ibis deliberately wanted to make things difficult for him. In recent years, because of rapid economic development and damage to the environment, ibises have no longer been able to live peacefully at the foot of mountains. They have been forced to move higher, to the middle elevations. If the environment at these elevations is destroyed, they will have no place to

The author and Liu Yinzeng (right) under the nesting tree of the crested ibises in Sanchahe

go, for it would be impossible for them to live in the thickly forested areas at the higher elevations. This is the danger now facing the ibises.

Liu and his guide followed the direction in which the ibis had flown, and continued looking for it. On May 23 they saw the ibis again and found some of its droppings. At this time they heard an unhappy story. A pair of ibises had built a nest in a big tree behind a house and bred two young birds, but the owner of the house decided to cut down the tree in order to make some money. Two young birds fell from the tree and died. The adult ibises did not want to leave the place; they just kept circling over Jinjiahe. The ibis that Liu Yinzeng saw might have been one of these. Noticing that the ibis always flew north in the evening, Liu Yinzeng guessed that there might be other ibises in that direction. He began a search that ended at Yaojiagou on May 27. There he saw an ibis looking for food in the fields. At first he thought it was the one from Jinjiahe, but a villager said, "They have built a nest in a tree and bred some young." Liu was shown the nest tree, where he found three nestlings. He decided not to go back to town but to remain in the ravine and observe the birds. Food was supplied to him once a week.

The arrival of people under the nest tree frightened the parent birds. They dared not return to feed their young, so the nestlings went hungry that day. At eleven in the evening, Liu Yinzeng was still out tape-recording under the tree when he heard something fall. Fearing that it was a young bird, he took out his flashlight and searched for a while, but he could not find it. The next day he went out to look again, but he found nothing. Later a boy came to tell him there was a bird behind his house. Liu Yinzeng hurried over and saw it lying on the ground, weak and hungry. He cut some river snails and frog meat into small pieces and fed the bird slowly. It revived a few minutes later, and he put it back in its nest, but not long after, it fell out again. The parents had ignored it, perhaps regarding it as a stranger because it had been touched by human hands and smelled different from the other birds. Each time it was put back, it fell from the tree again. Liu Yinzeng had to feed it himself and asked the Institute of Zoology for permission to send it back to Beijing to be raised there.

So the young bird, the tapes, the pictures, and other data were taken back to Beijing, and news of the discovery of the crested ibis spread quickly worldwide.

After Liu Yinzeng had "worn out iron shoes," as the saying goes, searching for the crested ibis in its preferred habitat, it turned up in unexpected places, forced by the destruction of its normal environment to seek new habitats. In light of this, the survival of the species remains precarious. The loss of even a single bird could tip the balance toward extinction.

Since Liu Yinzeng's discovery a major campaign has been launched to save the crested ibis. Steps have been taken to convince people of the importance of preserving the species, to reward anyone who provides clues to the whereabouts of the birds, and to punish anyone caught killing them. A vast amount of research has been done on the ecology and biological characteristics of the crested ibis. Preservation stations have been set up. Procedures have been adopted for long-term observation and food supply; land used for winter rice has been expanded and the use of pesticides has been limited. These measures increased the number of crested ibises from nine in 1981 to seventeen in 1984.

In May 1984 a special conference was held in Beijing to discuss ways of preserving the crested ibis, particularly the pros and cons of natural protection versus artificial raising and breeding.

The main advantage of natural protection is that it conforms to the laws of nature. The disadvantage is that with the ibis's extensive range of activity during July and August, human intervention, natural enemies, disease, and pollution are difficult to control. Besides, with so few birds to begin with, any natural increase would at first be quite limited. It is unlikely that natural breeding alone can save the crested ibis from extinction.

With artificial raising and breeding, there is no danger

from natural enemies, controlled feeding can help reduce disease, medical care can be provided if needed, and scientific research and international cooperation are facilitated. Attempts can be made to induce breeding by scientific methods. There is, however, no certainty that the ibis will breed under artificial conditions.

Balancing the pros and cons, the conference decided to adopt both methods. While the main emphasis will be on preserving the crested ibis in nature, artificial methods are to be tested on a few birds in order to increase their numbers as soon as possible.

Of the ten nests of ibis eggs observed in recent years, only five nests produced young. Among the twenty-one young, six died very early, two of illness and one of hunger. From these figures we can see that it will take extensive knowledge of environmental science, ecology, pathology, embryology, and genetics to increase the number of eggs laid and the incubation and survival rates.

From the poor bird that died, we have been able to learn a great deal through dissection and laboratory analysis. This new information should help us avoid such sad occurrences in the future. The efforts of people like Liu Yinzeng may save the precious crested ibis from extinction and help it flourish in our lifetime.

IN PURSUIT OF THE WILD ELEPHANT OF XISHUANGBANNA

I went to Xishuangbanna curious to learn why the few herds of wild elephants in Yunnan Province are the only ones left, when in earlier times numerous herds roamed the provinces south of the Yangtze River, especially in Fujian, Guangdong, Guangxi Zhuang, and Yunnan. Elephants were raised and trained for riding, for use in the fields, as beasts of burden, and as war animals. The latest recorded evidence of elephants in Guangxi dates from the seventeenth century. Now only about twenty elephants remain in Yunnan's Nangun River Nature Reserve and about two hundred in its Xishuangbanna reserves at Mengla and Mengyang. What caused the elephants in other areas to disappear?

We can learn something of the fate of these beasts from historical accounts, such as the *Moon and Mountain Collection* by Li Wenfeng of the Ming Dynasty, which includes this passage:

In 1547, in the reign of the Ming Dynasty Jiajing emperor, herds of elephants from Dalian Mountain trampled people's crops. Attempts to drive them away failed. Hu Ao, the county magistrate, and local officials led the villagers in an expedition to catch elephants. They created a fence of wooden boards three meters long held up by several people. As soon as the elephants entered the area of encirclement, the villagers closed the fence. Arrows were shot and spears hurled from a trench outside the fence to prevent the elephants from breaking out and running away. Then the villagers set fires in the area, for the elephants could not stand the heat. In this way they captured some dozen elephants.

The passage illustrates how human intrusion has affected the environment of wild elephants. The elephants trampled people's crops because heavy damage to the forests had made them homeless. Xishuangbanna still faces this problem. The government pays 20,000 to 30,000 yuan (about $5,000 to $7,500 US) each year to

A sand bath follows a river bath.

local peasants as compensation so they will not slaughter wild elephants.

Before going to Xishuangbanna, I read some of the classic works by experts on this topic and exchanged views with colleagues. In Xishuangbanna, I visited government bureaus and villages that had in the past raised elephants for the *tusi,* or headmen. I interviewed Dai elders, veteran hunters, elephant trainers, and former officials responsible for the headmen's elephants. Everything I learned led me to the general conclusion that two human activities are crucial to preservation of the wild elephants of Xishuangbanna: preservation of forests and, of course, protection of the wild elephants.

The relatively large area and sparse population of Xishuangbanna have helped protect wild elephants, but two Dai traditions are also responsible. The first is worship of the white elephant. Along with the peacock, dragon, and deer, the elephant is considered sacred and auspicious. The Wild Elephant Temple was built especially for worship of the elephant. Bright Elephant Mountain was named after the elephant. The Dais dance to the beat of a drum shaped like an elephant's foot. The elephant's image is seen everywhere—in their temples, in their bamboo houses, and in personal adornment. The first gift the Dais sent to Chairman Mao after Liberation was an elephant. In Dai culture the elephant is cherished and regarded as a friend.

The other tradition that has helped protect the elephant is the Dai people's esteem for the forest. Many areas, designated "dragon mountains," are considered holy. Trees may be planted, but it is a spiritual offense to cut them down. This practice has had the effect of sealing off hillsides and aiding forestation. Also, the consumption of wood in these hilly areas is low. Dai houses are built entirely of bamboo, from the supports and floors to the walls, stairs, and even kitchen utensils. For fuel their custom is to plant *Mesua ferrea,* a tree also called rose chestnut or "black heart," which burns well and sprouts again quickly after cutting. Thus there has been little need for people to go into the mountains to gather wood.

Because of these two traditions, the existence of wild elephants in Xishuangbanna today can be said to be an historical contribution of the Dai people.

ENTERING THE VIRGIN FOREST

Accompanied by Chen Darong, administrator of the local nature reserve, I set out on foot for the virgin forest in Mengla County, in search of elephant herds. We passed through five villages on our way: one Han, one Dai, one Yao, and two Hani. Our path followed a small river in the valley, sometimes on one side, sometimes on the other, and we often waded barefoot. Frequently we would find an old tree some hundred feet long lying

An elephantlike small-fruited fig tree

59

across the river, forming a sturdy but precarious bridge. Above such bridges the trees shut out the sunlight; below, the river roared. My guide was quite used to crossing on these bridges, but I certainly wasn't, and I sweated every inch.

The tropical forest was enchanting. Overhead were three or four tiers of green plants. At the very top, trees 100 to 130 feet high, called sky gazers, poked their small crowns through to the sky. The tops were visible only when we looked straight up. Below these trees was a variety of broadleaf trees, dense and thick, and beneath these, wild bananas and bamboo. There were also various symbiotic and parasitic plants and epiphytes. Together they formed a fantastic plant community. Despite Xishuangbanna's summery weather we felt chilly, as if we were walking through a green tunnel or along the bottom of a green sea. The roar of the water, the crack of twigs snapped by apes and monkeys, and the piercing calls of birds created an eerie atmosphere.

The wild elephants live in areas that combine features of the tropical rain forest with those of the subtropical

Wild elephants can be found in secluded spots at the riverside.

A herd of wild elephants in the rain forest

60

Spurting sand

seasonal rain forest. Along the way we carefully observed the environment. Because of the elephants' huge size, they are easy to track. Indeed, with feet resembling four hydraulic presses, elephants make ideal trailblazers. An elephant's trunk is as powerful as a tractor, able to haul a tree as much as a foot in diameter. The elephant's thick, tough skin protects it against thistles and thorns, and heals quickly if punctured or torn.

Elephants form herds of three or four to as many as forty-seven individuals. Each herd contains only one adult male, the rest being females and young. Male elephants that have been defeated in fights live alone, sometimes lame or missing a tusk, symbolizing their defeat.

The movements of these herds are regular. They do not have fixed dens but wander along a basic path covering more than a hundred miles. Some of the Mengla herds are international, wandering back and forth over the borders of Laos or Burma at intervals of ten days to about a month, sometimes influenced by the seasons. Experienced hunters can estimate when the herds will return.

One of two favorite places for these animals is the

so-called elephant pit, which has mineral salts in the water. The local people say that elephants are often followed there by sambur and muntjac, which in turn are likely to be followed by their predators, tigers and leopards. The elephants' other favorite place is flooded land, where they can bathe, splash, or rest.

They usually search for food at dawn or after dark. Their diet includes a variety of grasses as well as banana leaves, palm leaves, bamboo leaves, and bamboo shoots. They especially like the starchy pulp of a certain palm tree in the area. These trees grow tall and are usually fifteen to twenty inches thick. The elephant generally first sprays the roots of the tree with water from its trunk, then tramples the earth and bumps against the tree until it is able to pull it down with its trunk, strip off the bark, and get at the pulp.

I had been told that wild elephants were unlike the more gentle creatures seen in zoos. They can run as fast as a car and attack viciously, rolling their victims up in their trunks, then dropping them and trampling them to mincemeat, but they do not attack humans unprovoked. Chen told me repeatedly to be particularly cautious if I met a wounded single elephant or a mother elephant with young. If the elephant chased me, I should run in the opposite direction, he said, because its size makes turning around quite difficult. Unfortunately, we didn't see any elephants at all, and after wandering in the virgin forest for several days, we came out dog-tired and disappointed.

A NIGHT IN A HANI VILLAGE

Our next stop was a Hani village with a population of sixty-six situated less than two miles from the Laotian border. Two or three herds of elephants traveled back and forth across the border there.

We were welcomed by barking dogs, their number surpassing that of the human population—the moun-taineers like to keep dogs. Then the women and children came out. The men were dressed like Han Chinese but wore hats with red flowers on them. We stared at one another, full of curiosity. Living deep in the mountains about thirty miles from the commune seat, school, shops, and hospital, as well as the highway, they had never even seen their commune leaders, much less a visitor from Beijing. They seemed to be living in another world. They still use a slash-and-burn system of cultivation; have no writing, medicines, or vegetable gardens; wear coarse clothing they weave themselves; and eat upland rice and wild vegetables. Except for some silver jewelry worn by the women and children, they seemed to have little beyond the bare necessities.

Their primitive level of production and low standard of living have caused much damage to the forests. Each

A single tree can make a forest—a marvel of the tropical rain forest.

year these people burn large sections of forest as part of their system of cultivation. They use axes rather than saws to cut down trees to build houses, often abandoning large logs they cannot chop after cutting off only a few branches. The climate when I was there resembled that of Beijing in March or April, yet three fires were burning, one for cooking and one each for men and women to warm themselves. Whenever people were outside chatting, they had a fire burning at their feet. It is estimated that in a small village like this, tens or even hundreds of acres of wood are destroyed every year. After a decade or two, only burned tree stumps and bushes and terrible grass will remain for six or seven miles around the village, and the villagers will move to another location. They construct no agricultural structures, and plant only trees that can be used within two years. Basically, these Hanis are nomadic, as are the Yao, Jinuo, and Han people who have wandered into the mountains. (Members of these groups living out of the mountainous areas are not nomadic.) In addition, local peasants and nearby farm units destroy 16,000 to 33,000 acres of forest in Xishuangbanna every year. If this situation continues, the area is doomed, and Xishuangbanna, now rich and beautiful, may become a desert.

The while village was affected by my arrival. Hearing that they would be photographed, the villagers dressed up as if for a festival. The following evening the brigade leader called all the men together to hear the visitor from Beijing report on current affairs. I did not feel up to the task, but touched by their sincerity, I gave a report on protecting the natural environment, covering everything from the forests to the wild elephants, gaurs, gibbons, hornbills, peacock pheasants, mouse deer, and jungle fowl, and from nature reserves to the instructions of Premier Zhou Enlai, who had warned of coming dangers to the region in 1961. Finally I spoke about

how to protect the treasured land of Xishuangbanna. In some villages incomes had been increased and the forests protected by gathering medicinal herbs and cultivating edible fungus.

Although my explanations were quite ordinary, the audience listened with great interest. Afterward they asked me questions about the situation in Beijing and the world. They also asked about the elephants.

"Is it because the elephant is so huge that people should protect it?"

"That is one way of putting it," I replied. "There are various ways of looking at the value of elephants. They are scarce, found only in Africa and Asia, and their numbers are continually decreasing. Also, they are ancient creatures, existing in great numbers long before mankind. Hundreds of thousands of years ago there were elephants where Beijing is situated today."

"Why is the elephant so huge, with a long trunk and two big tusks?"

"This was not a matter of divine choice," I explained, "but the result of adaptation to its environment over a long period of time. Its huge size helps prolong its life. It is a plant-eating animal with few enemies, and its size, together with its enormous tusks, is enough to make even the tiger and leopard avoid it. The elephant breeds slowly, giving birth to a single calf after a gestation period of twenty months and averaging one pregnancy every six years, yet still it has not become extinct after thousands and thousands of years. Most of the big and tall plant-eating animals have long necks they can stretch up to eat leaves or down to eat grass. Only the elephant, whose head weighs over a thousand *jin* [1 *jin* equals 1.33 pounds], has no such neck. Instead, according to scientific research, in ancient times the elephant developed its long trunk in order to adapt itself to its environment. The trunk has a keen sense of smell, can take in water, can pick up a coin from the ground or a log weighing a thousand *jin*. The variety of its uses may be second only to the hands of a human being."

The villagers really came alive then and took turns adding their own stories to the discussion. Once a group of them had seen an elephant fall into a deep trench. The whole herd had come to its aid. The first elephant hooked its trunk around a tree; the second hooked its trunk around one of the rear legs of the first; the third and fourth elephants hooked their trunks around the leg of the elephant in front; the stranded elephant hooked its trunk around the rear leg of the last elephant in line.

Then the elephants pulled until the endangered elephant was out of the trench. Later, Chen pointed out the place where the elephant had been rescued, confirming the truth of the tale.

Although we sometimes had to use an interpreter, the conversation was lively. At midnight I had to suggest that we stop, because the following morning we were to go into the mountains to look again for wild elephants.

Common cleistanthus *(Anthocephalus chinensis)* is a fast-growing, tall, straight tropical tree. The wood of a ten-year-old tree is of a quality equal to that of a hundred-year-old Korean pine, a fifty-year-old Yunnan pine, or a twenty-year-old white poplar. It is known as the miracle tree.

A 230-foot-high Chinese parashorea of the Gurjun family *(Dipterocarpaceae)*

THE ROCK WAS MOVING!

After having been disappointed in Mengla, I was to go to Mengyang to investigate the problems of elephants and visit their haunts.

Since time was limited, I went to Sanchahe the after-noon I arrived in Mengyang, intending to turn back in the evening and make another stop the following day. Sanchahe was quite near the highway. A three-wheeled motorcar was sent by the nature reserve, and as soon as I arrived I was driven to the elephant pits.

They were similar to those I had seen in Mengla. Located in a secluded spot by a stream, they appeared more like marshland than actual pits, having been dug by the elephants with their feet and trunks. By each pit

Wallich pedocarpus *(Podocarpus wallichiana presl.)*, a rare living fossil

D. furbinatus Gaerfu, an evergreen tree of the Gurjun oil tree family in Xishuangbanna

A mouse deer—the smallest deer in the world

stood a thousand-year-old tree. Perhaps the elephants left the trees there to provide shade and seclusion.

As we were observing elephant and deer tracks, our guide, Tian, pointed to several prints as big as basins and said, "Look! The elephants were just here, and they can't have gone very far." My hopes fueled, I asked whether we could see them. He said they would pass by again the following morning and that we would see them if we arrived before dawn. Since food and a bed in the nearby village were all I needed, despite the driver's reminder that I had brought nothing with me, I decided to stay overnight.

I woke up with the first crow of the cocks and went out with Tian and another Dai youth, Yan Wendian, arriving at the pits just at daybreak. Unfortunately, the elephants had already passed, leaving only their tracks for me to see. This was not completely unexpected, as I had been warned in Beijing that I would probably never see wild elephants with my own eyes. Wherever I went I would be told that the elephants had just left.

Seeing my disappointment, my two guides had a long discussion in their own language. Finally Tian said, "Let's go back and have breakfast and then try another path. We are sure to see the elephants." I knew they were just consoling me, but I had no alternative.

Earlier we had walked along the river and streams looking for elephant tracks. Now we climbed the hill and went directly to the elephant path. From the path I could see that the elephants were more active and plentiful here than in Mengla, for here and there we would

Pig-tailed macaques

68

see elephant feces, broken sticks of bamboo, and traces of stripped bark. But these were not new marks. We made our way through the hills along the elephant path for five hours, listening to every sound.

At 2:20 P.M. Tian and Yan seemed to have discovered something simultaneously. They said softly but nervously, "Be careful! Don't make any noise!" I don't know whether it was excitement or fear, but my heart was thumping. All three of us lightened our steps. I tried to figure out what sign they were following but couldn't find anything. After a while Tian bent down and picked up some grass. "This was discarded by the elephants. You see the roots have been eaten." I examined it and saw that the grass was still fresh. About ten steps later we found a fresh pile of elephant feces. Tian touched it and it felt warm. The elephant could not be far away!

Inspired by this, we continued our pursuit for twenty-six minutes. Then Yan, standing on a slope, signaled to me to come over. I was too nervous to see anything. All I could see was a gray rock among the bamboo, about a hundred feet away. Oh, great heavens! The rock was moving! It was an elephant—a wild elephant! I had seen an elephant with my own eyes after all! I took my camera and rushed toward it. After a dozen steps or so I stopped and looked around. Tian and Yan were waving at me. Reluctantly, I headed back. Yan whispered, "Approaching it from below you'll be too obvious." Tian, too, warned me: "It is a mother elephant with her young. It might attack."

Yan determined the wind direction by tossing a handful of earth. As the wild elephant has a keen sense of smell, we chose a spot downwind and uphill from which to watch their movements. Sometimes our view was blocked by thick trees and bamboo, but the cracking sound of the elephants tearing through the bamboo guided us as we followed them. Finally, we could see that there were not two elephants but three, a baby elephant and its parents. The three ate as they walked. We followed them for about twenty minutes, winding through the bamboo. Then suddenly the long-tusked

A pair of rufous-necked hornbills

bull turned his head and looked as if he had seen us. Tian commanded, "Run!"

We all ran for our lives in the opposite direction until we reached the valley, far away from the elephants. There we sat on a fallen tree, gasping for breath. I grabbed the hands of Tian and Yan and thanked them. They said they were sorry I had been unable to get any photos, but between the shade from the trees and the tall, thick bamboo it had been impossible.

Later on I asked, "How could you tell the elephants were near?"

"By the smell."

"What smell?"

"It's hard to explain, but if you have smelled it many times, you can distinguish their odor from that of the gaur, sambur, and muntjac."

THE SIBERIAN CRANES DISCOVER POYANG LAKE

The International Crane Foundation had gathered evidence that the Siberian crane was on the brink of extinction with only two to three hundred left in the world. Then, in January 1984, newspapers in Beijing, Jiangxi, and Shanghai reported that up to seven hundred Siberian cranes had been sighted at Poyang Lake. I set off immediately.

A SPECIAL RELATIONSHIP

The Poyang Lake Nature Reserve in Jiangxi Province stands out among the many special bird sanctuaries in China because of its large number and variety of rare birds. Investigations by the Poyang Lake Bird Study Group revealed 150 species, of which 69 belong to the protection list of the migrant preservation agreement between China and Japan, and 12 are protected by the state. During our trip to the nature reserve we saw whistling swans *(Cygnus columbianus)* in Shahu (Sand Lake), white storks and bustards at Linggong Zhou, Siberian cranes and white-naped cranes at Dahu, and hooded cranes at Tanghu. Unfortunately, we did not see any black storks or common cranes, mandarin ducks, or red-crowned cranes, which are also scattered about the area.

According to fossil evidence, cranes, the most attractive birds in the reserve, have been on earth for 40 million years, much longer than man. They not only possess unique morphological and ecological characteristics, but are distinct genetically and are therefore of great value in the study of biological evolution, bionics, genetics, and aesthetics.

No one is quite sure when the first contacts between cranes and humans took place. The song of the crane is described in the *Book of Songs*, the first collection of poetry in China: "When the cranes sing in remote marshlands, their song can be heard in heaven." We learn from this snatch of poetry that the vast marshland

The Siberian cranes

has long been the crane's typical environment and that the crane's call is so loud and sharp that people can usually hear it before sighting the bird. The long necks and curving windpipes of cranes serve as trumpets, and when their necks and legs are stretched straight out in flight, they create a picture of elegant symmetry.

For over a thousand years in China, cranes have symbolized good luck, longevity, loyalty, elegance, and beauty, and have been depicted in paintings, sculpture, handicrafts, novels, poetry, and legends more often than any other animal. When Dr. George Archibald, a director of the International Crane Foundation, saw a red-crowned crane in China's Zhalong Nature Reserve, he said excitedly, "I feel as though I've found my family."

This feeling is not unique to bird lovers. In China's history many people have regarded cranes as among their closest friends. One of them was Lin Bu, a Northern Song Dynasty (960–1279) poet. In Hangzhou, I visited his residence on the bank of West Lake, where he lived in seclusion all his life, neither taking a government post nor marrying. His chief pleasures were to admire flowering plum trees and breed cranes, and he wrote many wonderful and moving poems about them. People often said that the plum tree was his wife and the crane his son.

This close spiritual relationship between man and crane, and the special ecological, economic, cultural, and scientific value of the crane, have inspired their protection and care.

THE SIGNIFICANCE OF NUMBERS

If you look at a standing Siberian crane, you see a body wholly covered with snowy-white feathers, but when the crane hovers in the air, you discover a ring of black feathers like two black cuffs at the end of its

Discovering Poyang Lake

wings. Its body is tall, slim, and graceful, and its song is flutelike. The British ornithologist Allan Hume, writing over a hundred years ago, described the Siberian crane as "beautiful and precious. It is the cream of all the birds. No matter what posture it takes, its head, neck and the line of its body are graceful and harmonious."

There are just two breeding groups of Siberian cranes in the world, the eastern and the western. The eastern group, which now contains about eight hundred birds, is scattered throughout the Kolyma River delta in the northern part of Siberia and the areas between the lower reaches of the Lena River and the Indigirka River. The western group, containing only fifty birds, was discovered by a tourist at the meeting of the lower reaches of the Ob River and the Irtish River in the Soviet Union. Every year when the Siberian cranes migrate, they pass through northeastern China and Hebei Province on their way to the middle or lower reaches of the Yangtze River. The western flock winters in northwestern India and Iran. According to Indian reports, there were seventy-seven Siberian cranes in India in 1972, sixty in 1976, thirty-eight in 1981, and thirty-five in 1982. Ornithologists were concerned over this steady decrease in the number of Siberian cranes and had great hopes of finding Siberian cranes wintering in China. In the winter of 1953 the Shanghai Museum of Natural History found two Siberian cranes in Anhui Province's Anqing region. Afterward, great but futile effort went into looking for the place where the Siberian cranes passed the winter. Not until the winter of 1980, twenty-seven years later, was a flock of ninety-one Siberian cranes discovered at Dahu, on the west bank of Poyang Lake, by Zhou Fuzhang and Ding Wenning of the Beijing Institute of Zoology. The following year, 140 Siberian cranes were found there, and in 1982 the Jiangxi Birdwatchers Group counted 189.

In 1984 a much bigger flock turned up, but how

Migrating from the north

In hot pursuit

many actually? Scientists' reports varied. Zhou Haizhong and Chen Bin of the Shanghai Museum of Natural History counted 457 Siberian cranes at Tanghu on the afternoon of December 30, 1983, including 76 young. They also observed fifty-seven families—three with two adults and two young; two with one adult and one young; and fifty-two with two adults and one young. Then, on the morning of January 8, 1984, they saw 154 Siberian cranes at Shahu, 15 of them young. That afternoon they found 19 Siberian cranes among the flocks of white-naped cranes at Dahu, giving them a total of more than 700. Two days later Feng Kemin of the Wildlife Research Institute in Heilongjiang saw flocks totaling more than 700 at Jiniu Mountain and Tanghu, and on February 15 about 840 Siberian cranes were seen at Dahu.

On the morning of February 25, Gan Shengyun, an expert from the Beijing Zoo who had studied cranes for thirty years, and I took a boat to Dahu to confirm the latest figures. We saw a dense cluster of Siberian cranes stretching for more than half a mile. Gan Shengyun took out binoculars to observe them carefully. She could find distinguishing features among the cranes and count the baby Siberian cranes with their small bodies and yellow feathers, but unfortunately it was a dark, rainy day and we were afraid of disturbing them if we moved in close for a count. From what we could see, the three sets of numbers mentioned earlier seemed reliable. Because some of the lakes in the area were dry, the cranes had had to move to where they could find food, and because it was nearing migration season, when they would travel as a group, various flocks had converged on Poyang Lake, resulting in the great numbers we found there.

What does this discovery of the world's largest group of Siberian cranes signify? Earlier findings reported only two breeding groups of no more than 300 altogether,

A small family

both located in Siberia. The discovery of 800 Siberian cranes at Poyang Lake means there must be at least a third group in the world, and their distribution is a new problem for naturalists to work on.

WHY ARE THERE MORE BIRDS AT POYANG LAKE EACH YEAR?

Three general answers to this question come readily to mind.

First, the ecosystem there provides an ideal wintering ground for waterfowl. Second, there has been extensive damage to lakes nearby. And third, there has been dramatic progress in protecting birds at Poyang Lake.

IDEAL WINTERING CONDITIONS.

Poyang Lake, the largest freshwater lake in China, lies in the north of Jiangxi Province at latitude 28° 20'–29° 50' north and longitude 115° 50'–116° 45' east. It is shaped like a large upside-down gourd, 31 to 44 miles from east to west and 105 miles from north to south. Five large rivers, the Ganjiang, Fuhe, Xinjiang, Yaohe, and Xiushui, flow into Poyang Lake from the west, south, and southeast, then flow north into the Yangtze. Every year these rivers deposit a large amount of silt at the mouth of the lake, forming sandbanks. The rivers also carry biological resources that enrich the lake and nearby swamps.

Poyang Lake is located in the wet monsoon region of the Asian subtropics. The average annual temperature is 62.6 degrees Fahrenheit. The lowest temperatures in winter are around 46.4 degrees. The frost-free period lasts an average of 270 days, and annual rainfall is 23.6 inches. The lake's water level changes drastically with the different seasons. From April to September the water covers a surface area of about 1,100 square miles.

A. *Hilsa* herring *(Hilsa reevesii)*

B. Catfish *(Leiocassis dumerili)*

C. Sucker *(Myxocyprinus asiaticus chinensis)*

D. Siniperca chuatsi

When boating on the lake, one has the feeling of being at sea. As the water level rises, fish from the Yangtze swim against the current into the lake to feed and to spawn. Sunshine is plentiful, and the water temperature is suitable for rapid breeding of plankton. The smooth-flowing water and abundant water plants provide the fish and other aquatic creatures with an ideal environment in which to grow. Of the 118 kinds of fish that live in or pass through the lake, 30 are considered to have substantial economic value. Rare fish include the China sturgeon, *Hilsa* herring, whitebait, and mandarin fish. There are also turtles, both hard- and soft-shell crabs, snails, clams, and various kinds of shrimp. These rich resources have been an economic boon to man and a plentiful food supply for the water birds.

The dry season runs from October to March. This is when migrant birds come to Poyang Lake to pass the winter. During this time the water covers a surface area of only 193 square miles. In many places the lake bottom is exposed, forming large expanses of muddy land and grassy islets. Sandbars and mounds of earth divide the lake into many small shallow lakes, from one to three feet deep. These shallow lakes full of fish, shrimp, and mollusks are a paradise for the water birds. At Poyang Lake we saw swans, mandarin ducks, gray-lags, and mallards swimming in the water while Siberian cranes and white-naped cranes waded in the shallows, bustards and black storks stood along the shore, and sea gulls and white-tailed harriers hovered in the sky. The birds shift positions depending on temperature, wind direction, water level, and food availability.

After spending time at Poyang Lake, the migrants are strong and healthy, ready to fly north to breed. They will have eliminated many sick fish, mice, and insect

Mandarin ducks

pests, safeguarding the ecological balance of the lake, and will have left feathers and a large amount of guano, good for the growth of water plants and plankton.

RECENT DAMAGE TO LAKES NEARBY.

A quick look at a map of China will show that most lakes are located along the middle and lower reaches of the Yangtze. Their topography, climate, water quality, and fish and plant resources make these lakes good places for birds to winter, so most of the migrant and resident birds in the country converge on this area. Investigations by ornithologists show that the distribution of cranes, storks, and other rare birds is around Hongze Lake and Gaoyou Lake in Jiangsu Province, Shijiu Lake and Caizi Lake in Anhui Province, Dongting Lake in Hunan Province and, of course, Poyang Lake in Jiangxi Province. But the rapid population growth and economic development of these areas, attended by uncontrolled disposal of industrial wastes and the use of pesticides and chemical fertilizers, are threatening the birds. According to a recent survey, using some of the most up-to-date technology available, the lakes of the Han River basin, known as the "thousand lakes," had

White stork

decreased from 609 to 309 over the past thirty years and the surface area covered by water had shrunk by 42 percent. The situation is the same at Dongting Lake. In 1825 the surface area was 2,316 square miles, but by 1977 it was only 1,057 square kilometers and getting smaller. It has been estimated that the famous Dongting Lake will be wiped off the map in less than forty years unless effective protective measures are taken very soon.

Once the ecosystems of such lakes have been destroyed, there is no question of water birds wintering there.

Poyang Lake is much bigger than Dongting Lake, its surrounding population density is lower, and it provides a better biological environment, so Poyang Lake has become a haven for migrants.

DRAMATIC INCREASE IN THE PROTECTION OF BIRDS.

After the killing of a large number of swans in 1983, which alarmed many people throughout our country, no guns were heard at the Poyang Lake reserve, nor did any wild birds appear in the marketplace. One man deserves a medal for this.

MODEL PROTECTOR OF BIRDS

When I was in Nanjing attending a meeting on the protection of cranes, I heard that a retired man—who was neither an employee of the nature reserve nor a bird specialist—had recently been named Model Protector of Birds. We met him on our trip to Wucheng, the center of the nature reserve. A strong, healthy sixty-two-year-old with a loud voice, He Xuguang seemed warmhearted, simple, and honest. He was carrying a great stack of documents concerning the importance of protecting the birds. From him we gained a better

Whistling swans

understanding of the changes that had taken place at Poyang Lake.

The people who had been living around Poyang Lake for generations had no thought of protecting the birds. They knew only that they could earn money by shooting them. Between 1976 and 1981 thousands of swans were killed, as well as other wild birds. At that time He Xuguang had no particular interest in birds, either. He was busy then beautifying his hometown by planting more trees.

In February 1982 he was asked to guide a group of scientists to Poyang Lake to observe the birds. Born and raised at Poyang Lake, he had herded cattle, fished, and logged there; he knew the rivers, lakes, and streams and the flora and fauna of the area like the back of his hand. When they reached Zhonghu and found flocks of swans there, Professor Deng Zongjue from Jiangxi University shouted with excitement: "This is another swan lake—another swan lake indeed!"

Surprised by this outburst, He Xuguang questioned

the old professor: "You are no longer young. Why have you come such a long distance to study birds here?"

The professor, who knew that He Xuguang was keen on forestation, answered, "If we don't protect the birds, how will the forests survive?"

This was He Xuguang's first lesson on birds.

No matter how bad the weather, he accompanied the scientists for several months as they moved from one lake to another. He gradually came to realize that Poyang Lake was a treasury of birds, and learned how to observe them, what their scientific names were, and what the relationship was between birds and their environment. His attention then turned entirely to birds.

Before the group of scientists left Poyang Lake, the old professor told He Xuguang that in a few days they would be sending someone to take pictures by plane, and he urged him again and again to take care of the swans in the lake and protect them from danger. He Xuguang accepted the task.

In December 1982, not long after the scientists left Poyang Lake, an event took place that shocked He Xuguang. Late one night he heard the sound of gunshots coming from somewhere along the lake. He immediately guessed that someone was hunting swans. Nothing could have made him more furious. He found the hunters and pleaded with them to stop. He told them about the importance of swans to mankind and the nature reserves; he even read to them portions of the Constitution that proved what they were doing was illegal. No matter what he said, they would not listen. He had to turn to the local government for help.

The local government used persuasion and education to reform the offenders and some of them were fined. It also classified ten large lakes covering 330,000 *mu* (almost 55,000 acres) as the Poyang Lake Migrant Birds Nature Reserve. After that, thanks to He Xuguang, the area was a paradise for migrant birds.

Birds are highly sensitive to their own safety. If a bird feels you will be kind, it may land on your shoulder and peck at food in your hand. If it feels you are hostile, it will fly off and never come back. The migrants at Poyang Lake must have sensed the changes there and come back, bringing more birds with them. This explains the miracle of being able to see eight hundred Siberian cranes there at one time.

Today, He Xuguang is an important person at Poyang Lake. Every day he travels between the lakes and grassy areas taking notes like a specialist on each rare bird he sees. If he finds a sick or wounded bird, he takes it home to care for it. He has rescued many wild birds and helped them return to nature. He has well and truly earned the title Model Protector of Birds.

THE
SECRET
CATHAY
SILVER
FIR

The Huaping forests, known as nature's secret hideaway, have an ancient and complicated topography; the climate is unusual and the scenery primeval. Numerous ancient and rare plants and animals flourish there. The key that first opened up this "secret hideaway" was the discovery of the Cathay silver fir *(Cathaya argyrophylla)*. It made the headlines in the international press in the 1950's, and for this reason Huaping became one of the first nature reserves in the country.

Members of the administration of the Huaping Nature Reserve on Mount Tianping told me that a 1979 survey by the Guangxi Institute of Biology had counted a total of 1,040 Cathay silver firs in six different localities in the region. The largest colony consisted of 300 trees, and the smallest of a single tree. I decided to focus on two areas: Yezhutang, with the greatest number of Cathay silver firs, and Wujiawan, where the largest Cathay silver fir in the world grows. Some people in the administration office said I could go to Yezhutang, but not to Wujiawan because it was too dangerous to travel there. A big snowstorm the previous winter had knocked down many trees and blocked off the road. From experience I knew that mountain folk usually look at city folk with a skeptical eye and overemphasize difficulties, so I insisted on going to Wujiawan. Reluctantly, they acceded. Actually, they had not been there for more than a year, and since it was seed-collecting season, they wanted to go. We decided that five men should precede us to clear a path through the forest and that an administrative officer should get a guide for us.

A PARTICULAR HABITAT

Our temporary base was in a desolate mountain hamlet on the Cu River, six miles from Mount Tianping. The hamlet consisted of a single two-story log cabin which had been built jointly by several research units in 1963 as a permanent observation post to study the Huaping

A black-naped oriole

plant ecology. During the ten years of the "cultural revolution" the post was abandoned, and the only person left was an old laborer who kept bees there. Later on, to "cut the tail of capitalism"—a phrase that was used often during the "cultural revolution"—even bees could not be kept and the cabin was locked up.

In spite of everything, the place looked just like Tao Yuanming's Land of Peach Blossoms. (Tao Yuanming, a poet of the Eastern Jin Dynasty [317–420], wrote *Land of Peach Blossoms*, about an idyllic place cut off from the rest of the world.) In front of the cabin was a clear mountain stream; on its left, a vegetable garden of about a third of an acre, lying fallow; on its right, a few banana trees standing tall and straight in the midst of a green bamboo grove. There were also two peach trees, colorful azaleas—more than thirty different va-

Huaping landscape

Cones of Cathay silver fir

Sowing Cathay silver firs

rieties—and plenty of wild fruit. If you were lucky, you could come across a lotus mushroom ten to twenty pounds in weight. The laborers told me: "If you listen carefully, you can hear the monkeys scream, morning and evening." Because of the height of the mountain and the density of the forest you could not hear the waterfall on the opposite side, which looked like a length of jade-green silk rippling down the mountainside, but you could hear the torrent of the Cu River without being able to see it.

While the laborers were cutting a path, my guide took me to see the Cathay silver firs between Shetangwan and Yezhutang. This was where the Cathay silver fir was first discovered and where most of them were growing. It was about two hours' walk along the mountain path from the Cu River. The Cathay silver fir grows at an altitude of 4,395 to 4,850 feet above sea level. Although this area is in an intermediate subtropical zone, summers are cool and there is snow in winter. All year round it is wrapped in fog, and precipitation and humidity levels are high. I looked around carefully.

Almost all the Cathay silver firs were growing on sheer cliffs and steep slopes. This was probably because they like sunshine and need a lot of moisture and good drainage. This rare and precious tree is always surrounded by vegetation that seems to grow with it. Standing at its side is the Japanese white pine *(Pinus parviflora)* or the Fujian cypress *(Fokienia hodginsii)*, dignified and majestic. There are almost always varicolored azaleas *(Rhododendron versicolor)*, a plant peculiar to the Huaping Reserve, and a carpet of mosses and lichens in acidulous humus. My guide told me that in Huaping Reserve almost all Cathay silver firs lived under these particular conditions. In Beijing, botanists spared no effort to transplant a few seedlings of the Cathay silver fir. Those seedlings are still alive in the greenhouse but have grown only a scant inch.

On the tall, beautiful Cathay silver firs I could see the traces of numerous scientific experiments. Labels were hanging from the branches and some of the branches were wrapped in plastic bags for air layering. Red strips of cloth and copper pieces were dangling from some of the big trees. My guide told me that the red color and the tinkling of the metal scared away the squirrels, which were doing too much damage to the trees by stealing the cones. Sometimes one could not spot a cone on a parent tree. My guide told me about the poor ability of the Cathay silver fir to regenerate naturally. Their viability and adaptability are poor; they grow slowly, bear fruit late, and have a low germination rate. Moreover, the broadleaf trees occupied a dominant position, forming a dense canopy that allowed little sunlight to touch the Cathay silver firs. Many plant diseases

The first Cathay silver firs artificially grown have blossomed

prevailed in the forest and serious damage was often done by wild animals, making it difficult for seedlings to reach full growth. In Huaping Reserve one still sees seedlings and saplings, but in Sichuan, Hunan, or Guizhou provinces one sees few seedlings or saplings. Without even the risk of human damage, these precious plants face the danger of extinction.

THE JOY OF DISCOVERY

The laborers had been working for two days but had managed to clear only one third of our road. I was getting impatient and decided to have the laborers go on clearing quickly while my guide and I followed them closely to make a crash expedition to Wujiawan.

At dawn we set out in heavy fog and drizzle, proceeding along the edge of a steep slope. At several spots the path was really hazardous. Above us the cliffs were lost in the clouds, while below us was the immeasurable expanse of the green gorge. The gray fog moved in on us at intervals, plunging us into darkness one moment and clearing up the next. The sheer cliffs were thick rock and thin soil. Many trees lay across the road, all of them decades old, if not a century old. Their twisted roots looked like fans lying on their sides. Some of the trees were really too big to be moved, so we climbed over them or crept underneath. Some served as a railing, giving us security as we clambered up.

All the time we could hear the roar of the Cu River, and finally, after two hours' walk and after descending several steep slopes, we reached the riverbank. The Cu River is an ancient stream with a steep drop. Both banks are lined with towering rocks, the woods on top obscuring the sky. On a dull day under a heavy fog the sun seems to set before noon. As there was no road on either side of the river, we took off our shoes and socks, rolled up our trousers, and stepped from stone to stone, wading upstream. The river is rightly called Cu River (meaning "rough river") after the big rough stones that cover the riverbed. With the water rushing past and moss covering them, the stones are quite slippery. In mid-November the water was cold, and wading barefoot for almost half a mile was torture. But greater hardships awaited us as we climbed ashore and up the hill. There was no road. The only indications of which way to go were the twigs that had been chopped off and the marks left on the trees by the laborers' hatchets. We were faced with a vertical crag. There seemed to be no way around and no room to maneuver. We had to abandon our walking sticks to leave our hands free to climb up; our only handholds came in the form of the thick plants and shrubs growing on the crag. In some places there was nothing at all to cling to, so the laborers had cut some forked branches or liana and hung them there for us to hold on to. My guide helped me climb as I clutched at a branch or liana. After almost two hours of hazardous climbing we finally reached the top of this terrifying crag. From there we descended to Baishuitan. A cold shower poured down and we were completely drenched.

Looking around me, however, I felt elated. The joy of exploration turned my thoughts to those who had first discovered this region. I had a definite goal and a ready route, and the laborers were there to clear the path for me and the guide to support me, yet I felt as though I had gone through untold hardships. What, then, of those scientists who had first discovered the Cathay silver fir many years ago? What was it like at that time?

Before climbing the mountains, I had paid a visit to Professor Zhong Jixin, deputy director of the Guangxi Academy of Sciences, who first discovered the Cathay silver fir. Coming down from the mountains, I hurried again to the Institute of Biology, but he had already left for Beijing to attend the National People's Congress. I followed him to Beijing and during an interval of the Congress had an opportunity once again to meet the seventy-four-year-old scientist. He was tall and straight, and in spite of his age his hearing and eyesight were still excellent. I guessed that in his youth he had been a

sportsman. I was right. He confided that he used to be fond of all kinds of ball games. When I asked him to tell me what it was like to make that first climb up to Wujiawan, he laughed and said, "I would love to see that place again, but my doctor won't allow me." These simple words almost answered my question. To be a distinguished biologist it is not enough to have the physique of a sportsman; it requires a passion for science and a complete dedication to one's work.

It was not by chance that twenty-seven years ago Professor Zhong and his team of researchers discovered the Cathay silver fir. Professor Zhong told me they had organized three expeditions before discovering it. At the time, even Wantian, which is today on a vital communication line, was only a remote village, very little frequented by people from outside; and Huaping, therefore, was hardly known at all. During the summer vacation of 1954, Professor Zhong took his students to collect specimens, and they went to Wantian. There an old man told him that before 1949 he had heard someone engaged in the illegal trafficking of opium to Guizhou Province say that some thirty miles into the mountains there was a mountain covered with ancient trees, all sorts of strange flowers, and rare plants. So, during the icy-cold winter vacation, Professor Zhong made a second expedition. Penetrating this time as far as Hongtan, he discovered that the region of Huaping was indeed one of nature's treasure houses. At the time Professor Zhong was deputy director of the Guangxi Branch Institute of the South China Institute of Biology, so he immediately sent a telegram to the Institute.

The following year a more important expedition, with Zhong as its leader, penetrated to the heart of the Huaping forests. A member of the expedition, Deng Xianfu, was the first to dig out a seedling. Exalted, he told Professor Zhong: "I have found a Fortune keteleeria [*Keteleeria fortunei*]!"

Zhong thought to himself: *The keteleeria cannot grow in this place.* As he looked more carefully, he found it did not look like the keteleeria. Maybe it was a new species!

So he hastened to ask whether Deng had found the parent tree. Deng said the mountain was too steep and the fog too dense.

At this moment the guide, Liu Jixin, provided a clue. He was a peasant who had fled Hunan Province before liberation in 1949, but he had hardly settled down when he was obliged to flee again to avoid being caught and conscripted. The Kuomintang sealed off his house, so he and his brother were forced to hide deep in the mountains and wild forests, making a living as hunters. Consequently, he had been to many places nobody else had ever seen. Liu told Professor Zhong that he had seen a tree that was neither pine nor fir but had something in common with both. It was big and tall and often grew along with the white pine.

Zhong felt more confident and set everybody looking for new species. Professor Zhong said to me: "You have been to Huaping now and know how difficult it is. At that time it was much worse—there were no footholds, no places to stay and rest, no paths man had ever trod. Our people fell ill, got hurt, were bitten by snakes . . . Ah, all that we went through."

In the end they found it. On May 16, 1955, they cut a branch with some cones on it from the southern slope of Mount Hongya. This was model specimen 00198, which I had seen at the Guangxi Institute of Biology. The specimen was later identified by the taxonomists Chen Huanyong and Kuang Keren as a new species of a new genus. Because its leaves resembled those of the fir and at the back of the leaves there were two silvery-white stomatal bands that glittered in the sunlight, the new species was named Cathay silver fir. The Soviet botanist Sugatchey just happened to be in China and saw the specimen of the Cathay silver fir. He found it had many similarities with a category of plant fossil found in the Soviet Union. The same kind of fossil had also been discovered in Germany and Poland. Only then did they realize that the Cathay silver fir was in fact a "living fossil." Ten million years ago, during the Pliocene Epoch of the Tertiary Period (in the Cenozoic geological

The largest Cathay silver fir in Haping

era), plants of the Cathay silver fir genus were widely distributed over the Eurasian continent. Then, during the Quaternary Period, owing to climatic changes, glaciers descended from the mountaintops and disaster befell the Cathay silver fir and other plants and animals. The tree was thought to have been extinct long ago and nobody expected it would so miraculously be rediscovered in China. Before the name *China* was known in the world, our country was called Cathay, derived from the Medieval Latin *Cataya*. To indicate that the Cathay silver fir is an ancient plant that has been found only in

China, scientists have given it the Latin name *Cathaya*. The greatest wish of many a foreign biologist who has visited China is to see the Cathay silver fir for himself.

ONGOING EXPERIMENT AND RESEARCH

Is the discovery of the Cathay silver fir the end of the search? Certainly not. The Cathay silver fir and the giant panda are both world-famous living fossils. These relict species survived through the centuries and are now showing signs of degeneration. Unless man intervenes, they may one day completely disappear from the face of the earth. The mission of scientists, naturalists, and concerned laymen is to find a way to keep them alive, which is an arduous and prolonged task requiring courage, insight, and vigor.

From the Cu River I returned to Mount Tianping, crossed another high mountain, and arrived at Hongtan. This was an isolated hamlet, the Experimental Station of the Guangxi Institute of Biology. Its task was to take the torch from the older generation of scientists and carry on research for conservation of the Cathay silver fir.

Hongtan is not the natural habitat of the Cathay silver fir, but seedlings have been cultivated there, and one finds seedlings of two years, four years, five years, six years. Although the work was interrupted for eleven years as a result of the "cultural revolution," there are still six trees that are seventeen years old, the tallest of which has reached a height of eleven and a half feet. Some saplings were cultivated through air layering. All these saplings and seedlings about equal the total number of wild Cathay silver firs in the country. I was told that a few years ago a foreigner offered to exchange a Trident airplane for one Cathay silver fir—but China has never used the Cathay silver fir as a medium of exchange.

The wealth of scientific achievement at this experimental station is precious indeed and has been hard won. People have tried to cultivate the Cathay silver fir in many places, but very few seeds have germinated and even fewer have survived. How, then, have the people here managed to succeed? I interviewed the man in charge, Shi Jinhua, forty-two years old, of Dong nationality and the only scientist at the station. He leads a team of seven, working all year round in this out-of-the-way mountain region. At Huaping Reserve for over twenty years, he qualifies for transfer to the Nanning Scientific and Technological Commission or to the Yanshan Institute of Biology in Guilin, but he is reluctant to leave this place, to leave the Cathay silver firs and the research work. His life may seem rather monotonous, caring for the Cathay silver firs by day and learning English with the help of a tape recorder at night, but it is a full life for him. As the Cathay silver firs have grown, Hongtan has gained in scientific esteem and Shi Jinhua has become an expert in his subject.

Naturally, he has not been alone in doing the job. A team called the Cathay Argyrophylla Study Group includes, besides the people of the experimental station, Huang Zhengfu, Li Ruigao, and Liang Muyuan from the Guangxi Institute of Biology. They have studied the Cathay silver fir together, published six scientific papers, and received an award for scientific and technological achievement from the Guangxi Autonomous Region. In addition, they have been commended as an "advanced group" by the city of Guilin.

They are a true "advanced group," working year in, year out, disregarding all personal discomfort. They have been collaborating closely, some at the institute, others at the experimental station. Most of their work has been done not in the laboratory or even at the station, but out in the virgin forests where the Cathay silver fir is hidden. Carrying their camping equipment and provisions, they have climbed cliffs and mountains, waded through

Jixin azalea, a plant special to Huaping

streams, and crossed ravines. In order to check the natural resources of the Cathay silver fir, they have searched through mountain wilderness. To determine the biological characteristics and ecological environment of the Cathay silver fir, they have conducted observations at regular intervals in predetermined places, regardless of the weather. They have collected an incredible amount of data, some of which could be obtained only after months or even years of observation. For example, only recently did the first generation of cultivated Cathay silver firs bear four male flowers, so only then did they learn that the Cathay silver fir takes as long as seventeen years to mature. But when the same tree will bear female flowers and when it will bear fruit—when, therefore, it will produce the next generation of Cathay silver firs—is, so far, nature's secret. Li Ruigao said jokingly, "We spend our whole life getting only a few bits of scientific information. It is the kind of research subject that shortens one's lifetime."

The experimental artificial cultivation is likewise an extremely complex and painstaking job. The Cathay silver fir bears very few seeds, which are very delicate, are difficult to store, and require for germination rigid conditions of which man has been ignorant until now. Hundreds of experiments in seeding at Hongtan and Yanshan have included using seeds from different trees,

Egrets and gray herons roosting on the same tree

sowing seeds at different times, using different methods of storing the seeds, different hormone treatments, different chemicals, different seeding substrates, and so on—all done to find the best method of germination. Through years of elaborate, careful experimentation the researchers finally succeeded in raising the germination rate from 4 percent to over 90 percent and published their findings.

Although they have been successful and have been given honors, they all assert with one voice that their work has only begun. The Cathay silver fir is a species with bright prospects. It is an evergreen, a graceful landscape tree, tall, straight, and precious. It makes high-grade timber for construction, shipbuilding, railroad ties, and furniture. Its bark, leaves, and cones possess medicinal properties, and its seeds contain a fairly high percentage of oil. In short, the Cathay silver fir is extremely valuable and can be put to many uses, but since it is labeled precious, rare, and endangered, it can't be considered useful at this time. Now that the riddle of its artificial cultivation has been solved, the next step is to find a way of making it grow faster. Air layering, pruning, and applying fertilizer and growth hormones are all possibilities. Another possibility is to use the slash pine *(Pinus elliotii)* as a stock in grafting the Cathay silver fir, a method successfully applied in Hunan Province. There may be other, better methods.

It is hoped that one day the silver fir, like the dove tree *(Davidia involucrata)* and the dawn redwood *(Metasequoia glyptostroboides)*, will become popular throughout the world. Pointing to the hillside, Shi Jinhua said to me proudly: "What we are aiming for is to transform the entire region here into a Cathay silver fir forest. After

A white egret nursing her young

that, we shall invite the trees to come down from the hills and learn to live in all parts of the world, so that they will bring immediate benefit to the people."

I laughed and said, "We shall probably not be around to witness this happy ending, but one day it will certainly come true."

A
RHAPSODY
TO
THE
SWAN

As soon as the Mongolian youths from the Jinguang Cattle Farm heard that I wanted to go to the Swan Lakes, they mounted seven Ili steeds, cracked their whips, shouted, and flew like arrows from the bow. Before I had a chance to think whether or not I should be frightened, these wildly exuberant young men had whirled me off into the heart of the Bayanbulak grasslands in China's northwestern province of Xinjiang. I heard the wind whistling in my ears, the youths cheering, and the horses neighing. The Tian Mountains were jumping up and down in the distance as the grassland underneath me slipped by like a bolt of dazzling brocade. In less than twenty minutes we reached the foot of Mount Baxilik. We slowed the horses to trot up to the summit. Lying flat on the edge of an overhanging cliff, I could not help uttering a cry of admiration. If a moment ago the race across the grasslands had excited me, the view of the Swan Lakes was even more thrilling.

Surrounded by the snow-capped East, West and South Tian Mountains, the Yurdus Basin stretched far and wide. This area of rivers, lakes, marshes, and springs, measuring almost four hundred square miles, is commonly known as the Swan Lakes. The grasslands were like a green carpet on which the Kaidu River zigzagged far into the horizon. Spread over this apparently infinite green were patches of white—the swans and egrets on the lakes, the flocks of sheep on the shores, the snow that topped the mountains, and the clouds drifting in the sky. The white looked pure, fresh, and smooth. The Swan Lakes indeed enchanted me. Only the seas and oceans could compete in vastness, yet they did not possess the lakes' riches; as for color, only the tropical rain forests could match them, but the rain forests lacked the lakes' clear perspective; in ruggedness only the Gobi Desert equaled them, but the difference between the two was one of death and life.

The Swan Lakes are a birder's paradise. The Xinjiang Scientific Expedition of 1981 found seventy-two different species of birds in the grasslands and peripheries. Among them were twenty species of water birds and twelve

A month-old cygnet

species each of wading birds and birds of prey; the rest were all songbirds. Thirteen species were registered as nationally protected birds, including the black stork *(Ciconia nigra)*, the white-bellied sea eagle *(Haliaeetus leucogaster)* and the whooper swan *(Cygnus cygnus)*, and twenty-nine species were migrant birds protected under the Sino-Japanese Agreement for the Protection of Migratory Birds. The songbirds and birds of prey were found mostly in the outer areas of the marshes or on isolated hills. The expedition's report summed up: "A great variety of species, countless numbers, a concentration of the habitat, and speedy growth and development are the four main characteristics of the bird resources in this water area." The family Anatidae is the most completely represented of the water birds with about one third of the Anatidae found in China; of these the diving ducks are by far the most numerous. Severe winters force most of the birds in the region, forty-four species in all, to be summer residents. In winter only seven species of birds remain, with a very small number of waterfowl that have, for one reason or another, not been able to migrate.

When I went to Bayanbulak, all species of waterfowl had finished breeding. They were molting and busy teaching their fledglings to fly, swim, dive, and look for food in preparation for the coming migration. I slowly scanned the scene with my field glasses. I had never seen such a variety of species and such a dense bird population. Black storks and common cranes were stalking across the grassland; bar-headed geese *(Anser indicus)* and brown-headed gulls *(Larus brunnicephalus)* were gliding over the lake; mallards and common redshanks were swimming about in the lake; Chinese cormorants and great egrets were standing on the riverbank; cinereous vultures were soaring overhead. All the time I could hear the warbling of songbirds. The most remarkable birds were, of course, the swans, because they were the largest. Their feathers were of the purest white and they floated on the lake with such grace and dignity that they were the first to strike the eye and naturally drew most attention.

My field glasses rested for a long while on a pair of

Dusk at Swan Lake

swans. One of the pair was cruising the lake, its long neck curved toward the water; the other was pluming its feathers by the lakeside. Their spotless white plumage, stately carriage, and leisurely movements infinitely enhanced the idyllic beauty of the scene. Lines by the Tang Dynasty poet Cui Hao came to my mind:

> The immortal of yore on a yellow crane left,
> Now lonely stands the Yellow Crane Tower.
> The yellow crane left forever and ever,
> And thousands of years the white clouds drift over.

An ornithologist had once told me that the "yellow crane" was in fact the swan. The Yellow Crane Tower is situated at Cape Huanghu on Serpent Hill near Wuchang. In the neighborhood one also finds Huanghu Hill, Huanghu Bank, and Huanghu Bay. *Huanghu* is the archaic Chinese name for swan. Depicting the swans hovering in the sky, Qu Yuan (semilegendary poet of the Warring States Period, said to have lived 340–278 B.C.) used the name *huanghu* to describe the swans soaring in the sky in one of the poems collected in *The Ballads of Chu*:

> With one beat of the wing
> The swan surges high.
> Mountains and streams
> Shrink as in dreams
> One more beat
> And on it soars,
> To the end of the earth
> Far into the universe.

Qu Yuan's description was no exaggeration; swans are the record holders of high flight among birds. Migrating from north to south, they sometimes cross "the roof of the world"—Mount Everest, or Qomolangma. I was reminded of the four swans flying abreast in a painting in the Urumqi museum that was originally one of the Tang murals in the Kizir Thousand Buddha Caves near Baicheng. I seemed to hear Tchaikovsky's *Swan Lake* ringing in my ears. I had seen the great Russian *prima ballerina assoluta* Ulanova dance *Swan Lake*. Now many other swans seemed to be dancing toward me. Which did I like better—the swan in nature or the swan in art? I could not make up my mind. Artistic beauty can be derived only from natural beauty, and natural beauty is enhanced by artistic beauty. My feelings were harmonizing the two, and I loved them both. But at last it seemed I loved natural beauty more.

Just as I was sunk in this happy contemplation, I caught sight of a third swan emerging from the thick grass. It was about the same size as the other two, but its feathers were a grayish color. I decided it was the young of the pair I had been watching. It waddled up to its parents, flapped its large wings, twisted its neck around to plume its feathers, then slowly moved into the water. Unless one looked carefully, one would not take it for a cygnet. In one month's time it would undertake the journey with its parents and the other adult birds. Where would they travel? To Poyang Lake in Jiangxi Province? Or to the south, to India, or to the Mediterranean in the west? Wherever they went, it would be miles and miles away. Again I marveled as I realized that this almost grown-up swan just six months ago was a mere cell visible only under a microscope, five months ago just an egg weighing a little over ten ounces, and four months ago only an "ugly duckling." Under the painstaking care of its parents, it increased five times in weight in two weeks, grew to nine pounds in two months, and by the time of the migration would weigh nearly twenty-two pounds. Such fast growth and indomitable life are indeed astounding. It is hard to tell at the moment how this rich endowment, preserved in the gene pool of the biosphere, will affect man's future development and exploits. Therefore, it is not only in the interest of nature, of ecological equilibrium, of aesthetics, but also in the interest of the future of mankind to protect the swan—to protect all rare birds, animals, plants, and flowers.

AN EIGHT-MONTH REST AND BREEDING PERIOD

There are five known species of swans in the world, and Bayanbulak boasts three of them: the whooper swan, the whistling swan *(Cygnus columbianus)* and the mute swan *(Cygnus olor)*. However, I saw only the whooper swan, and in great number. The whooper swan is also called the yellow-billed swan. The adult bird is entirely white except for its head and lore—the space between the eye and the bill—which are yellowish brown, while its bill and its feet are black with yellow at the base of the bill. It has a strong body so that it is able to defend itself. Its exceptionally long neck makes up for its inability to dive. The swan is typical of a species of bird that lives on open lakes and marshes. Among the migratory birds in Bayanbulak the whooper swan is one of the first to come and last to go, since it needs eight months to

Swan eggs, each weighing about 400 grams (a little less than a pound)

rest and breed. Two thirds of its life is spent in this region.

Every year in early April, even before the ground thaws, flocks of swans arrive from the distant south, flying in through the Ili Mountain valley and the Kaidu River gorge. Not waiting to recover from the fatigue of their long journey, they busy themselves with building their nests and breeding. To avoid being harassed or assaulted by man or beast, they settle their colonies on isolated isles or in shallow waters far from the shore. First they build a base for their nests out of silt and straw, slowly piling up the bits until the mound stands well above the water and is about six and a half feet in diameter. From afar it resembles a dune with a bowl-shaped top. But at times, fatigue or other factors cause the swans to turn away from their usual, elaborate building and make use of old nests or occupy the nests of other waterfowl. On several occasions ornithologists have seen swans occupy the nests of bar-headed geese and have noticed that while hatching their own eggs they also hatched those left behind by the geese.

About the middle of April the swans start laying their eggs, one every other day or so until three to seven eggs rest in each nest. The male and female take turns hatching the eggs and keeping watch. After about thirty days the downy cygnets break out of their shells. As soon as they open their eyes, they follow their parents into the water and swim around looking for food, coming back to their nests at night to keep warm.

Both adult and near-adult birds molt from mid-July to mid-August. At this time they are unable to fly and are easily captured, so they usually take refuge on open water and the banks of big rivers. The swan's diet is mainly vegetarian, consisting of such things as tabernae montanus bulrush *(Scirpus tabernaemontani)*, nut grass and its seeds, but also includes some animal food. By September they start to form their colonies, the biggest of which may number more than a thousand swans, descending from the sky like a big cloud and obscuring the sun when flying high. From October onward they

start migrating to the south in flocks. First to go are the colonies that did not breed; then those with young have to wait until the young are strong enough to undertake migration. During migration they fly mostly by night, probably as a precaution against birds of prey. Not until November do they all finish migrating, thus completing their cycle of life in this basin area.

If any young birds are not strong enough for the long migration, their parents spend the winter with them on the lakes. This happened very rarely in the past, but has occurred more frequently in recent years because people take their eggs. The swans then make up for the lost eggs by laying, hatching, and brooding more young. The shortened growth period of the late-born fledglings prevents their being strong enough by migration time, so their parents have to stay behind with them. The winter is harsh; the ground is frozen and food is scarce even if they take refuge near a still-flowing spring. More often than not, they die of hunger and cold or are caught by wolves or foxes. Very, very few can survive the winter on the Swan Lakes.

THE CHOICE OF A HOME BASE

Why have the swans chosen Bayanbulak as their home for the greater part of their life cycle? They come in great numbers. According to surveys, seven to eight thousand swans assemble here every year; in the past the number was several times that. What are the reasons for this?

The region provides three favorable conditions for swans, including many migratory species: climate, topography, and protective people.

CLIMATE. The swan breeds chiefly in high altitudes. Although Bayanbulak is situated at a northern latitude of 42° 28' to 43° 25', the temperature is markedly lower than in other regions of the Tian Mountains at the same latitude and height, because of the special topographical features of the basin area. The climate is distinctly influenced by the cold current of air that descends from the high mountains all around. In this vast basin, not one tree or shrub is visible. All sorts of experiments have been carried out, such as transplanting drought-resistant saplings on the northwestern slopes, which are sheltered from the winds. They were given the best fertilizer and ideal watering conditions. All in vain. During the first year these saplings remained green; the

Kaidu River, like a ribbon of hairpin curves

next, they turned yellow; and the year after, they all died. The summers are too short and cool; the winters are long and bitterly cold. The area is frost-free no more than twelve days in the year, so before these plants had time to complete their nutritive cycle, they were facing snow in June and frost in July. According to meteorological records, the average yearly temperature is 23.5 degrees Fahrenheit, while the lowest can reach 68 below. It is the second coldest region in the whole country, after Mohe in Heilongjiang Province. It is precisely this climatic environment that appeals to the swans.

TOPOGRAPHY. In Mongolian, *Bayanbulak* means "rich headwaters." Scores of rivers, large and small, twist through this vast flat terrain. In most places the water is no more than four feet deep, and everywhere isolated isles and sandbanks make it difficult for man or beast to pass through. On the shore near the waterfront one finds an abundance of marsh plants, such as cattail *(Typha latifolia)*, bulrush *(Scirpus validus)*, and sorrel *(Rumex spp.)*, and in the water, submerged plants, aquatic insects, worms, and fish. For habitation, cover, and food, the region is ideal for the swans or any other species of waterfowl.

PEOPLE. Bayanbulak is a most inaccessible basin deep in the Tian Mountains. In the past, there were only two passes; one led to the Yanqi Basin and the other to the Ili Valley. All other roads were just rough trails. Therefore the region was sparsely populated, chiefly by Mongolian herdsmen who followed a tradition of protecting birds. They particularly venerated the swan. A legend says that two hundred years ago, when the Turhut

Patrolling the shores of Swan Lake

Mongolian shepherds tending a wounded swan

Mongol tribe settled in this region, a white swan dropped down from the sky to the home of a poor child. The child took care of the swan, and when autumn came, the swan flew away, returning the following year with a few more swans. The child looked after them, just as he had the first swan. A sage approached the child and said, "You love and protect the swans; you are destined to a boundless future." The prophecy came true, as the child later became the chieftain of his tribe. Therefore, the herdsmen regard the swan as a beautiful messenger from heaven, a lucky omen, and a symbol of faith. When praying for a newborn child, they always say: "May you grow up like a swan, and may bright prospects lie before you."

The herdsmen never take the eggs of the swans, never catch a swan, and never harass the swans' nests. While visiting the Swan Lakes, I often saw swans not far from the yurts. They went about in pairs, sometimes followed by their young, as if they were part of the herdsmen's flock of domestic fowl. Actually it is not so strange. The yurts are always somewhere near the water and by the time the swans reach the age of courtship and marriage, they also leave the flock to look for a quiet sanctuary near the water. The herdsmen and swans trust one another and live in peaceful coexistence. Even a stranger such as I can see the swans up close, but only by approaching them slowly and on horseback.

THE SWANS' FRIENDS

Nowadays the swans' friends are not limited to herdsmen.

The Bayanbulak Nature Reserve was officially established in 1981 especially for conservation of the swans.

Before going to the Swan Lakes, I had attended a national conference of forestry department workers on the subject of nature reserves. The conference participants regarded conservation of nature as a strategic problem, drew up a plan for the development of nature reserves, and discussed the guiding principles, policies, and regulations for the establishment and management of nature reserves. The chairman of the conference, Vice-Minister of Forestry Dong Zhiyong, said to me enthusiastically: "I am totally concerned for all wildlife and the conservation of nature."

With the ever-growing demand for the conservation of nature, there will be more and more people dedicated to this cause. Those who impressed me most while I was at Bayanbulak were the local police. They have done much solid work to protect the swans, and prefecture has issued a circular commending their work. Besides generating publicity about protecting the swans, they have thoroughly investigated cases concerning harassment. For example, after confiscating five cygnets that had been captured by some local people a few years ago, they mobilized policemen and their families to look after the birds for more than three months and after-

ward released them in the Swan Lakes so that they could join the flock for migration. Soon after that they were told that a film studio had come to shoot some outdoor scenes and had kidnapped two little cygnets. The officer in charge, Wulumujiafu, rushed off to arrest the culprits. He traveled more than fifty kilometers and managed to recover one cygnet. The other had died.

Later, the police confiscated another cygnet from some local people. These two cygnets were very weak and ill and not able to migrate. If the birds were released back to nature, they would not survive, so it was decided that the deputy inspector, Hou Liangong, would be in charge of rearing the young birds. Hou's family vacated one room for the cygnets, regularly fed the birds, using their own rations, and gave them water to drink. It was no easy task for a layman to care for the wild birds. He had no idea of the swans' living or eating habits and did not know what to do when they fell ill. On top of everything the swans had enormous appetites, were noisy at night, made a mess of the room, and when they got lost, Hou would have to go looking for them at night with a flashlight. Nevertheless, Hou and his family over-came all those difficulties with the greatest sense of responsibility. Hou told me, laughing: "More difficulties lay ahead when we had to return them, because we did not simply return two ordinary swans but friends that had been with us day and night for one year. At the start they were hostile to us. They went on a hunger strike, struck us with their wings, and pecked at us. Later we became friends. As soon as they saw us, they would cackle at us, flap their wings, and come flying toward us from a very long distance. Then they had to go forever, and we were really sorry."

Not only human beings have feelings; animals can have them, too. One of the swans flew back after being released. They released it a second time, and finally the swan returned forever to nature.

My visit to the Swan Lakes was like a rhapsody with the cadence of poetry; with a melody as true, as good, as beautiful as the best landscape painting. There were notes of joy and anxiety, chords of passion and hope, mingled with the occasional dark phrase. I have written it all down, hoping that the rhapsody of the swan may last forever, always enchanting mankind.

AN AUDIENCE WITH THE GUIZHOU GOLDEN MONKEYS

More than two hundred years ago Mount Fanjing was a famous Buddhist shrine. People flocked there from Hunan, Hubei, Sichuan, Yunnan, and Guizhou provinces to pay their respects to the Buddha. On the remains of a stele, one may read: "Men and women come and go with their incense; it is just like a city."

Buddhists showed keen insight in choosing this location to pay homage to the Buddha. Mount Fanjing is the highest peak in the Wuling range in northeastern Guizhou Province. The mountains are magnificent, with immense forests blocking out the sky. Golden Summit, 8,178 feet above sea level, has not only clusters of exquisite temples but also many oddly shaped rocks with names like Treasured Rock, Mushroom Rock, and Ten-Thousand-Volumes Rock. Occasionally, because of certain physical effects of air and sunlight, a colorful light ring appears above the summit, and people are able to see their own shadows in the ring. The Buddhists believed that only those who had done sufficient charitable and pious deeds and were thus hopeful of becoming immortal could see the "magic light." All this beauty and mystery strongly attracted many visitors to the mountain.

In addition to the long, arduous journey to get there, the 6,500-foot perpendicular climb from the bottom of the mountain to Golden Summit was a painful trial for visitors. Golden Summit, clouds and mist curling around it, could be seen from a great distance, and travelers often thought they would soon reach their destination. But then they would scale another promontory . . . and another . . . and still Golden Summit would appear no nearer. This phenomenon was called by the local people a "rejoice-too-soon." When the traveler reached the top of the next hill, he found another "rejoice-too-soon." According to villagers, climbers experienced twenty-four "rejoice-too-soons" before they actually arrived at the summit. Weak-willed people often retreated in the face of such adversity, and even for the strong and devout it was a test of faith.

Unfortunately, this shrine has been plundered in at least three periods—the Ming and Qing dynasties and

Wanjuanshu ("ten thousand volumes of books"), an ancient rock formation

around 1949—so that all its relics and artifacts have vanished. The once widely traveled roads leading to Golden Summit are now covered with brambles and shrubs, and the stone slabs are green with moss.

Today, I climb the same path as those pilgrims who were determined to pay respect to the Buddha, and I am equally determined and just as much in awe, but hoping to achieve a very different goal. I have come in search of the Guizhou golden monkeys—animals so rare that their scientific value is beyond price. Fossils of the Guizhou golden monkeys have been discovered in Tongzi, a county not far from Mount Fanjing, indicating that the monkeys were living there as early as the fourth century. Only three to five hundred of these monkeys remain on earth, and all of them live in a small area near Mount Fanjing. It is unusual for a species of animal to be distributed over such a small area.

Few scientists have observed their habits firsthand or studied their way of life and their relationship to the environment; there are virtually no specimens, as only one hide exists outside China, and four hides and one skull within China. Not only is the scientific community unaware of them, but so is the general public. The Beijing Zoo had a brief exhibit of Guizhou golden monkeys, but no other zoo in the world has ever had them on display. They are living fossils, one of the world's most endangered species, and enjoy the highest possible degree of protection our country can provide.

BEFORE THE CLIMB

Getting an audience with the Guizhou golden monkeys is much more difficult than paying homage to the Buddha, because, however high and dangerous Golden Summit is, it *can* be reached. Before I even started climbing,

I was confronted with obstacles that at times seemed insurmountable.

At the Fanjing Scientific Conference in Guiyang which I attended before my trek, many people suggested I would not be able to locate the golden monkeys because the area is so great and the number of monkeys spread across it so small. Some people spoke of futile attempts in the past to find these monkeys. Ever since an Englishman bought a hide from a hunter in 1903, numerous naturalists, zoologists, and other zoo workers have gone to Mount Fanjing to look for Guizhou golden monkeys. For seventy or more years no one had seen a single one.

Thanks to the Guizhou Science Investigation Group, assisted by the Nature Reserve Administrative Office, the monkeys had been located. People from these agencies spotted the monkeys six times and took one male as a specimen. After following and observing them for quite some time, they were able to complete research on the monkeys' habitat, activities, feeding habits, and genetic

An arduous climb on Fanjingshan

Passing through an area of liverworts and low-hanging trees

go during the rainy season. His reply was very direct: "After days of rain the humidity is one hundred percent and conditions are extremely dangerous, since torrents of water often rush down the mountains. Last month a person from the television station was washed down the mountainside and almost killed. But even more frightening are the long-noded pit vipers, since this is the time when they are most prevalent. We are not afraid of the tigers or the brown bears, but these snakes have poisonous fangs more than one inch long and with the ability to pierce through several blood vessels at one time. When we go on an investigation, we always have ambulance drivers on duty and we always carry a wireless communication system. In spite of these precautions, several of our colleagues did not survive the wounds inflicted by these poisonous snakes. You must not go there by yourself."

His sincere advice kept me from going to sleep that night. After great mental anguish I finally formulated

structure. Xie Jiahua, who was in charge of the investigation, briefed me on the situation and told me that the monkeys lived in the broadleaf forests 4,500 to 5,900 feet above sea level. He also told me that in the region between the villages of Longjiaping and Yanhaoping there are perhaps three groups of golden monkeys that are easy to spot and whose activities are regular.

During the conference I also visited with the vice-leader of the observation group, Deng Fenglin, senior scientist in the Geological Bureau of Guizhou Province. I had intended simply to ask for directions, but unexpectedly Deng put a damper on my plans. "You can't go there now," he told me. "It is the rainy season. All investigators leave the area when the rains start. If you really want to go, you must wait until next March or April; those are the best times. Even cinematographers from a film studio have asked to go there, but I have advised them to postpone their trip."

I immediately asked Deng why I would not be able to

Studying the primitive forest

my own philosophical stand. If I did go in the rainy season, when other people were not present, I might actually be able to see more. Mountain torrents and the threat posed by long-noded vipers were definitely hazards, but one must experience some danger in life. I would just have to exercise caution at all times.

When Deng Fenglin heard that I had made up my mind to go, he surprisingly gave me his support and insisted on lending me a pair of leg wrappings to protect me from the vipers.

When I arrived in Jiangkou County, I was greeted by all the leaders from the Nature Reserve Administrative Office, but again I found the door slammed in my face. They informed me that there were no roads in the mountains, that there were no people living in the vicinity, and that, in addition to a guide, I had to hire a laborer to carry all my personal necessities up the mountain. The excursion would be quite costly. Because the budget of the Administrative Office was limited, it could not contribute any money toward my expenses. These people, too, alerted me to the dangers of searching for the monkeys alone. Clearly they were not interested in abetting my quest.

Smiling, I said to them: "You may think that writers on environmental problems are of little benefit." I had their attention, so I quickly continued, telling them the importance of articles concerned with environmental protection, emphasizing that without public support and the attention of government leaders, environmental protection would never be a high priority on the nation's agenda, and allocation of funds would always pose a problem. Exasperated, I demonstrated my extreme determination to pursue my cause by ending: "Even if I cannot get any assistance, I will go. Even if I lose my life, it is necessary for my work, and I will take full responsibility."

They were all moved by my earnestness and sincerity, and they agreed to locate two laborers and a guide. Yang Yieqin, who was in charge of scientific research, understood the significance of my work and thus sup-

ported me from beginning to end. He lent me a pair of leather boots and two bottles of medicine for injections in case I got bitten by vipers.

CLIMBING GOLDEN SUMMIT

The first day of our journey was devoted to climbing from the foot of the mountain to Golden Summit. While I was climbing, I often thought of the words scientists used to describe Mount Fanjing: ancient, unspoiled, and ecologically balanced.

I saw Mushroom Rock—a top-heavy structure that appeared to be on the verge of collapse. Ten-Thousand-

Mushroom Rock

Climbing Hongyun ("red clouds") Golden Summit

Volumes Rock was like a huge stack of books. Treasured Rock, among other metamorphic rocks, was inlaid with various kinds of smaller rocks. These formations are spectacular. According to isotopic determination, these strata are between 1 billion and 1.4 billion years old, more ancient than the oldest strata in Shennongjia, in western Hubei Province.

Throughout its geological history Mount Fanjing has gone through several major structural changes, along with weathering, erosion, and the chiseling of the glaciers. The ancient geological structure has nurtured the ecological system. There are still many ancient plants, such as *Idesia polycarpa*, ginkgo, Chinese tulip trees,

Dipteronia sinensis, Salix chienu Cheng, *Cercidiphyllum japonicum*, and *Tetracentron sinense* oliver. Similarly, the mountain harbors many animals, such as the civet cat, the serow, the South China tiger, and the Guizhou golden monkey.

When scientists describe Mount Fanjing as unspoiled, they aren't merely commenting on the purity of the chemical composition of the strata and the rocks but also on the clarity of the water. Most importantly they express the feeling that ancient Mount Fanjing, rising proudly beneath blue sky, touching the stars and the moon, has preserved its unique identity in the universe.

But why are the mountains so green and the waters so clear? Why are there no natural disasters? Why are the forests thick with *Idesia polycarpa*, Chinese tulip trees, Chinese hemlocks, and huge firs? Why have so many valuable and rare animals, including the Guizhou golden monkey, been able to survive here for several million years? Surely, all this has not happened by chance.

This area has always been remote, with few traces of human presence. Although it was once a center of Buddhist activities, the religion taught the people to respect the mountains, the waters, and the forests. Even though plunderers did much damage to the historical relics and many people were slaughtered, the area remained remote and grew even more isolated. As a result Mount Fanjing still does not have any roads, so its environmental protection is superior to other wilderness areas. The leaders of the Guizhou Provincial Committee once told me: "We will use helicopters before we build roads, and we will not support tourism." This decision demonstrates sound judgment.

As for ecological balance, anyone who enters these mountains will be impressed immediately, as this area is indeed an environmentally complete subtropical region. Forests cover 80 percent of the land, harboring more than 400 varieties of trees, 500 or more varieties of medicinal herbs, and more than 100 varieties of fungus. The area's 57 species of mammals, 173 species of birds, and 80 species of amphibians and reptiles live independently and survive in natural succession.

THE MAGIC LIGHT

At five o'clock in the afternoon, when we had climbed to the village of Huixiangping, not far from Golden Summit, we discovered the first traces of the monkeys. Everywhere twigs and leaves were scattered about, and occasionally we saw fresh monkey droppings. My companions informed me that we surely would have seen the golden monkeys if we had arrived the day before.

We continued climbing, finally arriving at our campground—Treasured Rock. We had just finished unpacking our gear when one of the laborers suddenly sang out, "Magic light! Magic light!" I looked in the direction of Golden Summit and saw a patch of orangy-rose-colored cloud approximately three hundred feet dis-

Golden Summit and the site of an ancient temple

tant. Unfortunately, the magic light was partially hidden by the summit itself and we could not see its beginning. As we were all exhausted from an entire day of climbing, none of us had the energy to climb the next rise, even though it was not very high; we had to place all our hopes on seeing this sight the next morning.

At the foot of the mountain it had been too hot to wear even a jacket, but on top of the mountain we had to put on our padded cotton coats and wrap up in our quilts. We hastily had something to eat and went straight to bed. The wind was a demon, disturbing our sleep the entire night. It beat on our plastic tarps and lifted our quilts like a hurricane. The cold penetrated to my marrow. Finally the wind blew away our tarps and other protective coverings, and we felt as if we had been abandoned in the path of a glacier. One of the laborers cursed out loud as he pulled his quilt over his head. We had not a minute of sleep all night.

Morning finally came, and we climbed to Golden Summit as we had planned, but the strong wind, cold rain, and dense fog drove away any interest in going farther. We could not even see clearly the famous scenic spots nearby, let alone the magic light. Hurriedly we placed our pot over a fire and cooked our meal so that we could get away quickly.

FIVE DAYS AND NIGHTS

After coming down from Golden Summit, we walked in the mountains for two days, finally arriving in the village of Yanhaoping, 5,478 feet above sea level. Here we had planned to build our station for observing the Guizhou golden monkeys.

In Yanhaoping conditions were a lot better than on Golden Summit. We had a triangular tent and a spring nearby; wind, rain, fog, and humidity were also not so severe as on Golden Summit. One of the laborers returned to the nature reserve offices after he had deposited the luggage, leaving us a "community" of three. One of us went to collect firewood, one to wash rice, and the third to make chopsticks. We tied wild vines to the trees for a clothesline, and we made a dinner table by placing a woven bamboo mat on a tree stump. Our situation was much like that of Robinson Crusoe, destitute on his desert island. Our soap, toothpaste, and toothbrushes were put beside the spring, and my watch and camera were hung on a tree where only monkeys could reach them. Our daily routine consisted mostly of cooking, talking, and looking for monkeys.

Our tent was hidden in dense forest, the haunt of the Guizhou golden monkeys. On all sides of our tent the forest was so thick with arrow and thorny bamboo that it was very difficult to enter. The tent was also overhung with evergreen and deciduous leaves of the mixed broadleaf forest. Most of the plants belonged to the Symplocaceae, the Celastraceae, the Fagaceae, and the rose families. This is the normal habitat for Guizhou golden monkeys, since they spend most of their time in the crowns of these big trees. The leaves, buds, bark, and fruit of the trees are their favorite foods.

Each morning after breakfast we all went out to search in the nearby mountains, keeping a sharp lookout for any movements of the monkeys and observing and studying the traces the monkeys left behind.

We stayed in the mountains for five days, with no sign of monkeys. During those five days and nights we were patient but anxious, hopeful but uncertain. The waiting made me feel quite lonely, but our talks around the campfire and the local Guizhou songs soon relieved this feeling. Whenever a stranger comes to the mountains, the people offer him cigarettes and tea. When they meet someone on the road, whether they know him or not, they always greet him and talk with him for a little while. This friendliness has more to do with the natural environment than with civilized society. Comparing the silence and peace here in the mountains with the noise and crowded conditions of the cities, I thought of words spoken by a man of the Guizhou Television

Broadcasting Station. He had once stayed in the mountains for three months, and after returning home, he said, "I seem to have just returned to earth. I want very much to hear people talk." People love nature, but they do not want to return to a primitive way of life. What many of us are searching for is a kind of harmony between society and nature—a big problem yet to be solved in today's modern world.

MY GUIDE

My guide, Zeng Fanrong, was in his fifties, a sedate, hardworking, hospitable man, most likely from a peas-ant family. He was transferred from a timber factory to this sanctuary, where he has worked for more than twenty years. When people from a research institute, a museum, or a television station come here to observe the Guizhou golden monkeys, he usually serves as their guide. He is familiar with every mountain, brook, valley, and small path in the area, and he has seen the monkeys twenty-five times, probably more than any other person in the world. Whenever he hears something stir in the mountains or the hoarse cry of the crows, he is able to find traces of the golden monkeys. Since he spends a good deal of time with natural scientists, he

A Guizhou golden monkey

has also learned quite a lot about living things. He knows not only the local names but also the scientific classifications of some animals and plants.

After we had camped out for several days, the Guizhou golden monkeys naturally became our most frequent topic of conversation. The local people refer to these monkeys as cow-tailed monkeys, because their tails are as long as their bodies and resemble those of cows. The Guizhou golden monkeys are very gregarious, traveling about in big and small groups. Zeng counted on his hands, then said to me: "I have seen a group of ninety or more monkeys four times; a group of more than thirty, five times; and a group of eighty, twice. Once near the village of Huixiangping I saw the largest group, nearly two hundred."

The Guizhou golden monkeys live in the trees, where they also look for food, play, and sleep. They occasionally climb down to the ground to drink water or search for additional food, but they always return to the trees. Like the best gymnasts, they can span six to ten feet in one leap—even farther if jumping from a high place. Before jumping they huddle up, then extend their limbs and, with a burst of energy, spring forward. As the weight of their bodies hits the branches, they use the resiliency of the branches to spring to the next tree. The monkeys can also grasp a branch with one arm and swing from one spot to another.

Dawn and dusk are the monkeys' most active times. When they move, all the branches sway, making it look as if the monkeys are everywhere on the mountain. They are well disciplined. While some of the monkeys look for food, others climb trees, jump about, and chase each other, often coming to blows, or fight for a chance to hold the babies—which causes the baby monkeys to scream. When the "duty officer" discovers anything out of the ordinary, he gives a loud cry and immediately silence reigns. In only a few seconds the monkeys, sensing danger, have all disappeared. After retreating several hundred yards, they gather together again, summoned by one of the monkeys. If a monkey is caught in a noose or a trap, the others come to try to break the rope with their teeth in order to rescue their friend.

A PRECIOUS PHOTOGRAPH

The guide also told me how two golden monkeys were once captured. I compared what he told me with what I knew of the monkeys that had been in the zoo, and it gave me a more complete picture. The first monkey was caught in 1967 in the village of Jinzhanping, to the west of Mount Fanjing. The monkey had come down from the mountains in order to find gourds to eat. One of her forelimbs was caught in a trap set by an old man, and she became quite an unusual captive. The government bought the monkey from the old man and sent a telegram to the Institute of Zoology. In a few days the monkey was flown to Beijing.

The second monkey was caught in 1970 in the village of Panxi, south of Mount Fanjing. Some Guizhou golden monkeys had come down from the mountain to eat pea seedlings, and a gluttonous one was left behind, to be found later by a small child. When people heard of this discovery, they sent four dogs to chase the monkey. Guizhou golden monkeys are very quick in the trees, but on the ground they move rather clumsily. This monkey was now completely surrounded by the dogs, who were barking viciously at him. The monkey was at a loss as to what to do, so he simply gave up and sat on his haunches. The people immediately advanced and captured him. The monkey was exhibited in the local area for a week before the villagers asked Beijing to fetch him.

The first monkey, a female, weighed seventeen pounds. After some time in the research institute her weight increased to eighteen and a half pounds. In early 1968 she was sent to the Beijing Zoo, but she was not exhibited. This particular golden monkey was relatively docile and could be walked outside on a chain. She ate food from her keeper's hand, and she did not exhibit fear of people. After some time her health improved significantly, and in 1969 she mated with a Shaanxi Province golden monkey. After a normal pregnancy she gave birth the morning of March 15, 1970, to a female baby, which the mother cared for until it grew up.

In the summer of that year the second Mount Fanjing monkey was sent to the Beijing Zoo. A male, he was placed next to the female monkey. These two captives became friends in adversity, exchanging greetings with each other through the bars of their cages. They began to develop a very friendly and intimate relationship. Before long the female monkey went into heat; she not only wanted to be near the male monkey, she often lay down on the floor to seduce him. The keepers then put them together in the same cage. They cohabited for five days, during which time they copulated frequently. They always remained physically close, and the male monkey not only showed his love for his mate by often combing her fine hair, but also sometimes hugged his little stepdaughter.

Suddenly the male monkey's appetite shrank drastically. His keeper, worried that the monkey's constitution had not yet recovered fully from the long journey and that the monkey had not thoroughly adjusted to staying in captivity, decided to isolate him from the female monkey. Not long after that, the female monkey suffered from abdominal distention and a digestive disease because her feed had been too concentrated. She died unexpectedly after having lived three years in captivity. In January 1974, after barely four years in captivity, the male monkey also died. Even the crossbred descendant of the female monkey did not live long enough to mate. All that remains is a photograph of the pair with the baby, taken during the five days in which they were together. This photograph has become a very special document.

Except for less than a month, when the male monkey was exhibited to the public at the Beijing Zoo, these monkeys were kept in a compound in the outer suburbs of Beijing. Therefore, only one in a million people in the world has been able to see these rare and precious animals. I had gone to a lot of trouble, traveling such a long distance and camping in these remote mountains and wild forests, in the hope of being fortunate enough to see the Guizhou golden monkeys.

THE SIXTH MORNING

After five days (actually eight, counting from the day we first started to climb Golden Summit) we were all a bit apprehensive but tried not to show it. At daybreak the next morning we went directly outside without cooking breakfast. As I had injured my toes in climbing the rocks, it was very painful for me to walk. My two companions urged me to remain in the observation station and watch for movement and listen for sounds while they went into the forest.

Several other observation stations existed in the area, each a platform constructed from tree branches and wild vines, supported by the limbs of tall trees. The deck provided a place where television crews could film the monkeys. A simple ladder hung down from each platform. I climbed to the highest of these platforms, about sixty-five feet up. This high above the ground, swaying gently, I felt as if I were in a light boat bobbing in a green sea. Over an expanse of several hundred *mu* (one hundred *mu* equal sixteen and a half acres) I could see broadleaf forest. In the far distance I could also see miles of mountains in the clouds. Holding my breath, I looked closely for any movement in the dense foliage. Whenever I heard an unusual sound or saw some leaves fluttering slightly, my ears and eyes immediately located the source of the sound or movement. But always it was only a bird singing tirelessly or the breeze blowing the leaves. When I became weary from standing, I sat down to relax, and when I grew tired of sitting, I lay down on the platform, thinking: *Golden monkeys, where are you?*

Can it be that I have to return disappointed? No! I am determined to wait. I vow that I shall not go back without seeing you!

I stood up again. By this time the sun had risen above the horizon, dodging in and out of the white clouds behind the distant mountains. The sun looked huge, incredibly red and beautiful. In a moment the east was bright with the rosy clouds of dawn, and the entire world was reveling in the sun's embrace. The sun, nurturing the green mountains and rivers, the boundless forests, the golden monkeys, and also our fellow human beings, seemed to me then the source of all energy and wisdom, and the greatest, most beautiful, immortal mother.

At that moment, when my imagination was running wild, I caught an unusual signal. "What?" I asked out loud. "What is it?" In the grove, about sixty-five feet from where I was posted, I saw the tree branches shaking violently. My heart immediately leapt into my throat, just as if I were a devout Buddhist who had seen the magic light. Next I heard the sound of footsteps, and I called out in a soft voice, "Zeng, come up here quickly!"

Zeng immediately climbed up to the platform and looked in the direction in which I was pointing. He shouted, "Golden monkeys! Golden monkeys!"

Yes, it was the golden monkeys, and at last, at long last, I was to see them.

Most of the monkeys were advancing in a row, moving rhythmically like a band of humans walking quickly. They clambered ahead in good order toward the northwest side of the hill. I could see them clearly now: gray hair, long tails. Zeng imitated the monkeys' cry and one of them stopped in its tracks, turned its head, and looked to see where the sound had come from. While I was busy counting the monkeys, Zeng shouted again:

Fairy Bridge on Golden Summit

A beautiful scene in Fanjingshan Nature Reserve

"Spotted monkey! There is a spotted monkey in the group!" What he meant by "spotted monkey" was a monkey that had white spots all over its body. I looked in the direction he had pointed, but as we were not very near the monkeys, I could not see the spotted one. Zeng told me this was the group of thirty he had seen before. I had just counted thirty monkeys.

We climbed down to follow the monkeys for more than an hour. The group was bustling with noise and excitement, snapping the branches of the trees, making sounds like puppies. Because the forest was too dense, the bamboo too thick, and the monkeys constantly moving about, it was extremely difficult to make close observation and impossible to take good pictures. The monkeys left us farther and farther behind, until finally we lost sight of them altogether.

Back in our tent, I grasped Zeng's hands tightly and said to him excitedly: "We can now return home."

Zeng smiled and said, "I do not know how many times people have come from faraway places to search for the golden monkeys, but I do know that few people have actually seen them. The scientific observation group that came last year were the first outsiders to see the monkeys; the second were several people from the television station who came earlier this year. The third is you."

GOOD NEWS

My audience with the Guizhou golden monkeys concludes with two encouraging observations. The first is that the trapping and killing of them have nearly been stopped. According to incomplete figures, four were killed by traps in 1963 and one in 1964, one was captured alive in 1967, one was shot to death in 1969, one was caught alive in 1970, two were shot to death in 1975, and three were killed by traps in 1977. The male and female who were captured alive were the two sent to the Beijing Zoo. From these statistics it can be seen that people often set traps in the mountains for other animals but accidentally caught golden monkeys instead when they came down from the mountains, perhaps looking for food. There is no record of people deliberately hunting them, so their numbers have not been reduced substantially by man. Furthermore, after Mount Fanjing became a nature reserve, the local people were notified that the "cow-tailed" monkeys were to be protected by the country, and anyone caught killing them would be sent to jail. No longer can people kill them as in the past, though some research institutions wish to accumulate several more specimens and hope to capture more monkeys in order to breed them artificially. My opinion is that we should not be overzealous in studying these monkeys but should allow their numbers to increase through natural propagation.

The second observation is that, according to the local people, there are many young ones among the monkeys, indicating that this species is exhibiting a tendency to survive. If we continue to do effective work in protecting them, taking good care of the monkeys as well as the forest in which they live, the Guizhou golden monkeys may possibly remove themselves from the imminent danger of extinction. Surely, this is everyone's hope.

THE WUYI MOUNTAINS— A LIVING LABORATORY

We circled upward through lush vegetation for some sixty miles, until we finally reached Mount Huanggang, the highest summit of the Wuyi mountain range and also, at an altitude of 7,078 feet, the highest point in southeastern China. The view was breathtaking. We were lost in the clouds, mist stretching far below. I sensed the closeness of the sky, while the earth seemed far, far away.

The whole Wuyi range is bewitching—undulating hills, crisscrossing mountain streams, dense forests, vast green waves of pine and bamboo, and everywhere birdsong and the fragrance of flowers. But on top the scene changes dramatically. Meadows full of day lilies in autumn become a golden carpet. Here and there are Taiwan pines *(Pinus taiwanensis)*, barely reaching a person's shoulder, their growth stunted by conditions of soil, climate, and ultraviolet radiation. Though decades, if not centuries, old, these pines appear to be saplings. On the southern slope near the summit stands a coppice of precious Chinese littleleaf box trees *(Buxus siruca)*. The wood, sold as a rule by the *jin* (1.33 pounds), is used for carving. This mountain range straddles the border between Fujian and Jiangxi provinces for 340 miles, and one must conclude, as Mao Zedong did in a poem, that "the landscape here is beyond compare." The nature reserve is on the Fujian side, although the Jiangxi side is also densely wooded and rich in resources.

The Wuyi Mountains form a natural protective screen against cold currents from the northwest, at the same time retaining the warm, moist airstream that comes in from the sea and gives this region its humid, often misty climate with plenty of rainfall. Moreover, there are great differences in altitude, and the geological structure is unusual. There are high mountains, deep valleys, and small basins. Each landform's particular situation, with slopes facing in different directions, creates a special environment that provides the proper conditions in which different organisms may flourish. The region abounds in all kinds of subtropical-, temperate-, and frigid-zone plants. Specimens already collected comprise 190 fami-

lies, 799 genera, 1,715 species, and 12 varieties, including more than 50 species of rare trees, among them the Chinese bretschneidera *(Bretschneidera sinensis)*, the Chinese tulip tree *(Liriodendron chinense)*, Oyama magnolia *(Magnolia sieboldii)*, and Huangshan mountain magnolia *(Magnolia cylindrica)*. There are also numerous mosses, lichens, fungi, and algae. Because it is so out-of-the-way, the area has suffered relatively little disruption from man. Forest cover is as high as 92 percent, of which 98 percent is natural forest, including vast stretches of primeval forest where man has scarcely ever penetrated. This is unique, not only in Fujian Province but throughout the country.

Such an abundance of plant life inevitably leads to a rich variety of insects, amphibians, reptiles, fish, birds, and animals. They are too numerous to mention, even if I limited myself to the rare and indigenous species. I shall just quote some simple figures: In China we have 32 orders of insects, 31 of them here in the Wuji Mountains; 160 species of reptiles, 61 here (including 16 species of venomous snakes); more than 1,100 species of birds, 165 here (5 exclusive to the area). Therefore, it is no exaggeration to say that the Wuyi Mountain Nature Reserve is both a window and a living museum of biology.

TWO WELL-KNOWN PLACES NOT ON THE MAP

Guadun and Dazhulan together consist of no more than a few households and are almost impossible to find on the map, but both these names have long been known to many people at home and abroad. If Chinese biologists ventured to the Wuyi Mountains and bypassed those two places, they would be said not to have been to the Wuyi Mountains. As for foreign biologists, they might not have heard of Fujian Province or the Wuyi Mountains, but very few would not know of Guadun and Dazhulan, because both sanctuaries produce model specimens that are displayed in famous museums all over the world.

Both Guadun and Dazhulan are situated in the heart of the Wuyi Mountain Nature Reserve at an altitude between 3,200 and 5,900 feet above sea level. The unusual topography has produced an extraordinary collection of rare and precious flora and fauna. The French priest Father David Armand first discovered Guadun 180 years ago and returned with a collection of specimens. The following year he published a thesis on some new species of birds. The Englishman La Touche, hearing the news, sent some people to look for the place. They searched three years before finding it, but brought back a great number of bird specimens. On this basis La Touche wrote *A Handbook of Birds of East China*. A German zoologist spent 375 days not long ago collecting specimens at Guadun and Dazhulan and came away with 160,000 insect specimens that are now kept in a West Berlin museum. He is still studying these specimens and writing about the new species. Clifford H. Pope, a zoologist at the American Museum of Natural History in New York who specializes in amphibians and reptiles, also came here to collect great numbers of frog and snake specimens and wrote a number of papers on the new species he found. He concluded: "Guadun is the key to research of Chinese amphibians and reptiles."

I visited sixty-five-year-old Fu Qifa, the last inhabitant to move out of Dazhulan. He and his father and grandfather had all worked as guides for the foreigners, carrying their specimen cases and collecting specimens for them. Some of those foreigners worked as missionaries among the mountain population and bought specimens from them. They would pay 10 *fen* (100 *fen* equal 1 yuan, or about 25 cents) for an insect and 1 yuan for one of scientific value; and if the villagers managed to catch two rare species, they would give them a double-barreled shotgun as a reward. Fu further told me that his grandfather had once shot a completely black tiger for the foreigners. I did not quite believe him, so on my return to Beijing I consulted the zoologist Tan Bangjie, who told me that there were indeed all-black tigers.

Because of their religious zeal, their money, and adventurous spirit, those missionaries were the first to raise the curtain on the hidden treasures of the Wuyi Mountains.

A SCIENCE OUTPOST DEEP
IN THE MOUNTAINS

In Sangang, six to nine miles from Guadun and Dazhulan, deep in the mountains, two buildings have recently been

Guadun, a paradise for Chinese and foreign biologists

erected. Signs in front of them read: ADMINISTRATIVE OFFICE OF THE WUYI MOUNTAIN NATURE RESERVE AND SCIENCE OUTPOST OF THE FUJIAN PROVINCIAL SCIENTIFIC AND TECHNOLOGICAL COMMISSION.

The Administrative Office now has a staff of sixty-three who engage in conservation of the natural environment and natural resources. They are also in charge of organizing the few inhabitants of the region to carry on productive activities that do not disrupt the conservation of nature, such as tea cultivation, apiculture, and the manufacture of bamboo articles. In addition they have set up a laboratory for research closely related to their conservation work.

The Wuyi Mountain Multiple Science Observation Group is a multidisciplinary scientific observation unit incorporating more than 130 specialized personnel from 38 different departments. They cannot possibly stay here throughout the year, but come in turns to carry out their observations during specific seasons. The Science Outpost, however, maintains a permanent staff which is responsible for looking after these visitors. The Provincial Scientific and Technological Commission allocates as much as 200,000 yuan (about $50,000) annually to the post to provide accommodation and four cars for transport, as well as incubators, refrigerators, air-drying equipment, microscopes, telescopes, and protective equipment for the use of visiting scientists. The Science Outpost is filled regularly with experienced scientists as well as young amateurs in biology. Wearing straw hats, shin guards, and protective socks and carrying nets and snake forks, they go deep into the mountains to catch snakes, frogs, and insects and look for animals, injecting the vitality of scientific activity into the still, green Wuyi Mountains. They have made significant findings. According to incomplete statistics, just recently they have discovered one new family, one new genus, forty new species, and nine new subspecies.

Scenery in the Wuyi Mountains

Let me give an example of the importance of such work. The white woolly aphid is widespread in the cane-producing areas of Guangdong, Fujian, Guangxi, and Yunnan. This pest prevents the sugar cane from growing well, causing the farmers to suffer great losses every year. If insecticides are used, they not only affect the quality of the sugar but pollute the environment and harm the useful insects as well. It seems that in the Philippines a kind of parasitic wasp is the natural enemy of this kind of aphid. People searched the four provinces for this aphid wasp, but without success. Just as they were considering whether it would be possible to introduce this wasp from the Philippines, Professor Zhao Xiufu and his team of scientists discovered the aphid wasp in the Wuyi Mountains. Now they have taken it to the biological control laboratory of the Fujian Agricultural Institute for indoor cultivation and breeding. If

Professor Zhao Xiufu (left) collecting specimens in Wuyi Mountains

they succeed, it will make an important contribution to the sugar cane industry. Professor Zhao said, "According to the most conservative estimates, there are at least one hundred fifty thousand different species of insects, and of these, no more than one to two thousand, a mere one percent, are destructive insects. As for the ninety-nine percent, they are worth looking into. In this respect the Wuyi Mountains are indeed an inexhaustible supply of natural enemies."

The scenery at Jiuqu, in the Wuyi Mountains

A DEDICATED TEAM

Heavy rains forced me to seek shelter at the Institute for the Prevention of Snakebite Injuries. Our hosts were most hospitable. They fed us dried mushrooms and tender slices of bamboo shoots they had collected themselves, and fish fresh from a mountain stream. They served us the famous Wuyi tea *(Thea sinensis* var. *bohea)*, which is much in demand in Britain. I was deeply touched by their warm hospitality but even more moved by the conversations I had with them during my two days and two nights there.

I found out that this institute differs from other research institutes in three ways.

First, the fourteen people who work at the institute all actually take part in medical research. No one does only support work. From the director to the accountant, the storekeeper to the chef, everyone does two jobs at a time or in turn. Besides their medical research, all of them collect specimens, rear snakes, plant medicinal herbs, carry water, cook, wash clothes for their patients, and so forth.

A second way the institute differs from others is that with the exception of the director, who is in his early fifties, the staff is composed entirely of unmarried young men and women between the ages of sixteen and twenty-six. Even the director, whose marriage broke up during the disastrous years of the "cultural revolution," had not yet remarried. They live a close, united, busy collective life. They rise, have breakfast, start and finish work, hold meetings, study, go to bed, all by the whistle. In order to concentrate all their energies on becoming more proficient in their jobs, they even made a rule that cards and chess could be played only on Saturday evenings and Sundays. Within this collective two take the lead and set an example for the others. They are Zhang Zhen, the director, quite mature both politically and professionally, and Wen Meiyu, the deputy director, a pacesetter in China's new Long March toward modernization, and well known throughout the country. Following their example, the others have all put their hearts into caring for their patients and doing their scientific research.

While I was staying at the institute, I had an unexpected opportunity to see the strength of this collective. Three days of heavy rains had caused torrents of water to stream down the mountainside, breaking one of the dikes behind the institute. Waters rushed toward the back wall of the snake farm, and soon a section of the wall threatened to collapse. Nearly a thousand venomous and nonvenomous snakes were kept at the farm, the most valuable property of the institute. Now they could be washed away in an instant. Without waiting for the command of the whistle, all the young people and their director threw aside umbrellas, shed coats, and jumped into the current. The water reached their waists as some of them dredged the watercourse and others built a dam. They struggled for half a day, but finally succeeded in saving the snake farm they had so painstakingly created.

A third way the institute proves unique is in the high priority the staff gives to application of its research. During the past few years staff members rescued hundreds of working people from death by combining methods of modern, traditional, and herbal Chinese medicine, in the process accumulating fairly complete case histories. They have developed some very effective drugs, including Wuyi Snakebite Antidote. They have also extracted all sorts of scientifically valuable snake venoms,

Zhang Zhen and his assistants observing a long-noded pit viper raised in captivity

Wen Meiyu, the first woman snake doctor in China

concocted the medically highly effective Wuyi Mountain Snake Wine, succeeded in breeding various venomous snakes by imitating natural conditions at the snake farm, and made a start in solving the problem of breeding moccasins *(Agkistrodon acutus)*. By going into the mountains at regular intervals to collect specimens and observe the habits of different snakes, staff members have become quite familiar with the distribution and ecology of the reptiles in the Wuyi Mountains and have learned about the beneficial and harmful effects of the snakes and how to exploit them. Their achievements are based on solid fundamental knowledge and are, therefore, most valuable.

Their hard work and dedication to their patients have won them high esteem among the local population. Although there are many amateur "snake doctors" in

A. Horned toad

B. *Eremias argus argus*

C. A crested kingfisher

Red-billed magpie

the region, patients suffering from snakebite come to the institute from hundreds of miles away, brought by tractor or on stretchers. Among them are snake charmers as well as people who sell snake antidotes and cure snakebite. Once these people have been bitten by a snake, they cannot help themselves and come to the institute to be cured. Many patients arrive covered with blood, screaming and groaning in pain, but leave fully recovered, profoundly grateful, often with tears in their eyes. To show their gratitude, recovered patients have offered money, presents, and silk banners of commendation, but staff members always refuse these gifts. So, not knowing how else to thank them, patients have forged strong ties of friendship, visiting during holidays and

Huanggang Mountain, the highest mountain in southeastern China

festivals and bringing with them snakes and other rare animals they have caught. As a result, the king cobras *(Naja hannah)* that have been found in the Wuyi Mountains are preserved at the institute, along with a complete series of specimens of two-horned, three-horned, and four-horned toads, from egg to tadpole to full-grown horned toad. The research work of the institute has had the full support and help of the local inhabitants, who thus share in its achievements.

The Wuyi Mountains are truly a living laboratory for scientific research.

SILVER PHEASANTS, GREEN DESERTS

What is more nerve-racking than waiting for someone you are not sure will even show up? I looked at my watch—3:40. For more than two hours I had been crouched behind some bushes on the forested mountainside, hoping to catch a glimpse of a beautiful species of wild pheasant: the silver pheasant.

I am not a zoologist, and it was only when I started to write about the national nature reserves that the differences between creatures in the wild and caged animals in zoos became clear to me. Compared to wild animals, the listless, pitiable denizens of zoos seemed scarcely more alive than the stuffed specimens in a museum. A famous Qing Dynasty artist once said, "All my life I've disliked keeping pet birds in cages, yet I kept them there just for my pleasure. Is this really reasonable, to make *them* follow my way?"

My desire to see animals in the wild had grown stronger and stronger, like an eagerness to see close friends no matter how long the journey or how great the risk. So when I heard that an ornithologist was studying silver pheasants in the field, I asked him to take me with him. He had set up observation posts near two feeding stations stocked with corn. We trekked to the first post, where he told me to hide in the bushes, urging me to keep completely silent: If I made the slightest noise, the silver pheasants would not come. Then he went off to the second post.

I waited patiently. After a few minutes five or six mosquitoes began flying in circles around me. It was so quiet in the forest that their buzzing sounded like airplane engines, very threatening. They obviously disliked the strong insect repellent I was wearing, but they were not about to pass up an opportunity to sample my blood. Some began to bite my hands. For fear of disturbing the silver pheasants, I did nothing but blow at the mosquitoes one by one.

How long should I stay here? I wondered. *Will they come at all today?* I decided to wait until half past five. If I stayed any longer, I would have to make my way down the mountain in darkness.

A blue whistling thrush

Suddenly, with a soft *coo*, *coo*, a silver pheasant appeared less than a hundred feet away, as if it had popped out of the earth. It was a male. He strolled toward my hiding place and looked around, then began pecking at the corn.

I observed him carefully. His body was one meter—more than a yard—long. His crest and underparts were dark-blue. His white upper parts were lined with black, his long tail feathers making his body look twice its actual size. His cheeks were scarlet, and he seemed to be wearing a pair of pink high-heeled shoes. From every angle he was a beauty.

He pecked at the corn as he walked. When he had had enough, he turned his head and preened his feathers. Then, uttering a series of low notes that resembled the combined sounds of a hen, a pigeon, and a frog, he flapped his wings so rapidly that he seemed to be encased in a blurry white globe. I was disappointed not to be able to take a picture of him, but by that time the light in the forest was too dim.

Li Bai (Li Po), the famous Tang Dynasty poet, was fascinated by the silver pheasant's beauty. When his best friend, Hu Hui, sent him two silver pheasants, he wrote him a poem in return:

Please allow me to buy two silver pheasants from you
　　with two pieces of white jade.
The silver pheasants are as white as white brocade; their
　　snowy whiteness makes me ashamed of my own
　　appearance.
In the jade lake their profiles are reflected as they preen
　　their feathers on the bank.
The cold moon is quiet while they sleep; in the morning
　　they take a leisurely stroll by the lotus pond.
I'd like to have the birds to play with while sitting in the
　　Jade Mountains.
It was very kind of you to give them to me; in cages I'll
　　take them home.

In another poem about silver pheasants, written early in the Ming Dynasty, Yang Ji describes their habitat, their behavior, their elegance.

The mountain turns white when the birch-leaf pears are
　　in blossom.
With the arrival of the white pheasants in spring the
　　trees turn green.
Too hastily the orioles and swallows fly past, not notic-
　　ing the idle guests among the flowering shrubs.
They are unhappy when the dew moistens their newly
　　grown feathers at dawn; what they like is standing
　　beside the Xiang River catching the reflection of
　　the setting sun.

Now, for the first time, I understood the enjoyment that bird lovers find in watching birds. I had observed a silver pheasant little more than three hundred yards off

Dinghu Mountain Nature Reserve on the Tropic of Cancer is a popular tourist attraction.

the road, in the Dinghu Mountain Nature Reserve, just fifty-two miles west of Guangzhou (Canton) and twelve miles east of Zhaoqing. How marvelous to be able to see such a rare and beautiful creature in a well-preserved forest ecosystem so near these busy cities!

A RICH BUT FRAGILE ECOSYSTEM

Dinghu Mountain Nature Reserve is unique in several ways. Despite its name, it is near several large population centers, it has a low elevation (its lowest point being ninety-two feet below sea level), and, most important, it is a green haven in the Tropic of Cancer, a portion of the globe that usually calls to mind a zone of deserts.

If you look at a map of the world, you will see that the land on both sides of the Tropic of Cancer—encompassing the Indochina Peninsula, the southern part of the Arabian Peninsula, northern Africa, and the southern part of North America—is almost all desert. This is because the climate of the region is dominated by the northeast trade winds which blow from higher to lower latitudes. As the winds sweep south, temperatures rise and humidity drops, making rain unlikely and turning the land into tropical deserts.

Here and there, however, the topographical interplay between land and ocean has created exceptions. One is China's Xishuangbanna region, located in the southern part of the Asian continent, bordering on Laos and Burma, and near the Indian Ocean. Another is the Dinghu Mountain region, located on the east coast of the Asian continent near the Pacific Ocean. Though these regions lie on the Tropic of Cancer, the wet, hot monsoons from the ocean bring abundant rainfall, creating what are known as monsoon rain forests.

Scientists regard Dinghu Mountain as an indispensable resource for biological varieties ranging from the subtropical to the tropical, a storehouse of genes for breeding and genetic engineering, and a living nature

A. A beautiful silver pheasant

B. Young egrets coming to rest here

C. The chestnut-flanked white-eye

museum. The northernmost of seventeen research stations established for the study of tropical ecosystems, the area was one of the first to be set aside as a nature reserve. In 1979 the executive bureau of UNESCO accepted Dinghu Mountain as part of an international network of forest reserves. Together with the Changbai Mountains in Jilin Province and the Baiyin Xili Pasture of Xilingolmeng in the Inner Mongolia Autonomous Region, Dinghu Mountain is a vital component of a joint research project called Man and the Biosphere, sponsored by the United Nations.

Dinghu Mountain is higher in the northwest than in the southeast. In summer the southeast monsoon brings abundant rain from the Pacific Ocean, while in winter the mountain's proximity to a tropical sea exerts a moderating influence on temperatures, despite frequent cold waves from the north. Because the climate ranges from monsoon tropical to subtropical, temperatures vary greatly over the year, and the region has distinct dry and wet seasons. The yearly average temperature is 69.8 degrees Fahrenheit. In July, the hottest month, temperatures average 82.4 degrees, with a high of 98.2. January is the coldest month, with an average just under 55 degrees Fahrenheit and a low of 28.4. It rains an average of 151 days a year, mostly in the spring and summer; annual precipitation averages 75.9 inches.

Reflecting Dinghu Mountain's location and climate, its vegetation shares the characteristics of both tropical rain forests and the broadleaf evergreen forests of the subtropics. On my own sojourns to Dinghu Mountain, I counted more than a hundred different kinds of tropical and subtropical vines, or lianas, sixty of which were woody-stemmed varieties. Some three hundred yards to the south of Qingyun Temple, I saw vines as thick as the mouth of a rice bowl, swinging in the wind like the bodies of huge dragons. I also saw thirty varieties of epiphytes (plants that live nonparasitically on other plants) growing in the trees.

Natural forests make up about one fourth of the 17,000-*mu* (about 2,800 acres) nature reserve of Dinghu

Long, thick lianas, characteristic of a rain forest

Stemmed fruit

Black spinulosa cyathea, renowned as a living fossil

Mountain. The major trees *(Castanopsis chinensis, Schima superba, Canarium pimela, Canarium album, Erythrophloeum fordii, Syzygium rehderianum, Syzygium levinei, Aporosa yünnanensis, Cryptocarya chinensis,* and *Caryota ochlandra)* are typical of the varieties found in northern tropical forests. Scientists classify these forests by their degree of stratification, ranging from three to seven levels. The highest level consists of trees sixty-five to one hundred feet tall, with separation at the crowns; the next highest level comprises trees twenty-six to thirty-six feet tall, with their crowns bunched together. Below these come bushes, young trees, and ground vegetation such as grasses, ferns, mosses, and lichens. Although most of the trees range in age from thirty to one hundred years, there are a few specimens, including some Indochina dragonplums, several centuries old, as well as many young trees no more than ten years old. Where climatic conditions are favorable, different types of trees grow close together and flourish, having established a cooperative relationship despite different spatial and nutritional requirements.

Over many years of investigation and research, a total of 1,700 varieties of higher plants have been discovered on Dinghu Mountain. Many, such as *Lindera chunii* and *Ilex tinghushaensis,* are rare trees that grow only in China. *Cyathea podophylla* and *Erythrophloeum fordii* are precious ancient plants. Among the useful plants found here are 320 varieties suitable for lumbering, 70 varieties that can be used for oil, 40 varieties for starch, 110 varieties for fibers, 60 varieties for tanning materials, and 900 for medicines.

The various plants and rich food resources in this nature reserve provide home and breeding grounds for 38 species of mammals, 177 species of birds, 27 species of reptiles, and 11 species of amphibians.

Dinghu Mountain's forest ecosystem—with its multilevel structure of evergreens—makes efficient use of light energy, and its biological productivity is high. The soil has a good chemical composition and a complex underground structure with deep drainage that helps conserve water. In addition, microorganic activity helps speed the return of nutrients to the soil, thus restoring fertility.

The natural forest forms a stable ecosystem, marked by complex space and nourishment structures, and highly specialized subsystems. It has a great capacity for self-regulation, utilizing both positive and negative feedback.

Waiting for food

The forest can defend itself against severe natural calamities and can withstand a large amount of selective cutting. But at the same time the natural forest is fragile in the sense that it is very hard to restore once destroyed, even when efforts are made to re-create the ecosystem artificially. The barren hillsides outside Dinghu Mountain's natural forests could not be successfully reforested despite thirty years of trying, mainly because of soil leaching and erosion due to high temperatures and heavy rains and the distinct wet and dry seasons characteristic of a transition zone between tropical and subtropical climates.

A SPECIAL PLACE IN THE NATURE RESERVE

On the eastern slope of Three Treasures Peak a fenced-off area forty meters long and fifty meters wide (approximately half an acre) has been set aside for experiments. Nobody can enter this area without permission.

With respect to topography, soil, and vegetation, the two thousand square meters of land in this enclave are virtually identical to the land outside. The only difference is that human interventions can be controlled. Researchers come at certain intervals to observe, take notes, and analyze the plants in order to learn more about their growth patterns and life cycles. Within this enclosed area a plot twenty meters square (about 4,300 square feet) has been set aside for close observation. Here, every small change in the ecosystem is recorded. Ten nets measuring two square meters (or 43 square feet) each have been hung among the trees to collect falling leaves. By counting these leaves and measuring their caloric content, the utilization rate of solar energy in the forest can be calculated. Each June and September, carbon dioxide is measured in order to analyze the process of photosynthesis. The enclave on Three Treasures Peak is a living archive and an outdoor laboratory that will help researchers answer more and more questions about the forest ecosystem as time goes by.

In the early 1950's, teachers and students of the Biology Department at Zhongshan University conducted a detailed investigation of the vegetation on Dinghu Mountain, with special emphasis on the relationship between environmental factors and the distribution of species and varieties. Their findings were summarized in a paper called "A Study of Plant Communities of Dinghu Mountain in Gaoyao, Guangdong Province." Twenty-five years later, Wang Bosun and Ma Manjie wrote an article, "The Successions of the Forest Communities of Dinghu Mountain Nature Reserve," comparing more recent surveys with earlier records.

This research on the development of forest communities over time has led to new understanding of the life cycle of trees from their early to later stages and has shown how forests evolve into optimally stable ecosystems under undisturbed natural conditions.

Setting aside a small piece of land for a long period of experimentation and observation has proved to be a valuable project indeed, providing us with the scientific knowledge needed for the preservation of the trees of the region and giving us hope for "naturalizing" artificial forests so that once again they may flourish.

HAINAN'S RICHES

Only a small finger of Chinese land reaches down into the tropics, and Hainan Island covers nearly 42 percent of it. With an area of 12,430 square miles, Hainan Island is slightly smaller than Taiwan and represents only 0.35 percent of China's total land mass. Despite its small size, it is probably China's richest area in the diversity of creatures in its ecological system. For years it had been my dream to visit there.

The island supports more than 4,000 varieties of plants, 344 species of birds, 78 species of mammals, 37 species of amphibians, 104 species of reptiles, and more than 600 species of aquatic creatures that have commercial value. Also, on the continental shelf around the island are large mangrove forests and coral reefs, creating an underwater farm stocked with numerous shrimp, fish, and cowries. Seven nature reserves have already been established on the island in order to preserve this treasure house, and more shelters are being built.

THE MYSTERIOUS FOREST

My first stop was the mangrove forest reserve in the village of Dongzhaigang, located in Qiongshan County. The forest, covering an area of more than 6,400 acres, is only a two-hour drive from the city of Haikou and stretches along the edge of the continental shelf for more than thirty miles. From a high promontory on the beach one can see tracts of dark-green "sea forests" in the distance, looking like green clouds floating on the gulf, its tributaries, and small rivulets. These are the mangrove forests, a unique ecosystem.

Actually, the so-called mangrove forest refers not to one particular species but to a community of trees typical of continental shelves in tropical and subtropical zones. There are twenty-three families and eighty-one varieties of plants in the world's mangrove forests, of which China has sixteen families and twenty-nine varieties. The village of Dongzhaigang alone has twelve families

A gibbon in the forest

and nineteen varieties of mangrove trees, representing 60 percent of China's species.

Mangrove forests are composed not only of strong, tall trees but also of low shrubs and lianas—high-climbing woody vines. The ground is covered with a lush growth of green plants and grass. Underground and on the surface, thick supporting roots, snake-shaped and board-shaped, crisscross. These profuse twisted roots and gnarled branches form what appears to be a green Great Wall, keeping out the wind, blocking the silt, and protecting the embankment. Despite fierce winds, rain, and the rising and falling of the tides, the mangrove forests stand rock-firm to protect the fertile farmland within this natural dike.

The workers in this reserve informed me that on July 22, 1980, typhoon number 7, accompanied by violent rain and high tides, lashed ferociously at the northeast coast of Hainan Island. The people of Dongzhaigang village built two dikes to protect the farmland from this strong typhoon. Since most of the mangrove trees in front of the east dike had been cut down in order to reclaim land from the sea, the dike was not able to bear the force of the typhoon and the tides. It broke in eighty-four places, damaging 3,598 feet along the coast. The farmland inside the dike was badly destroyed. The west dike, however, was protected by the mangrove forests. Only thirteen places were breached by the flood for a total of 643 feet, and the farmland there was only slightly damaged.

Many organic substances are present in the water in which mangrove forests thrive. Mild winds and low

Seeds of *kandelia candel*

A bird's nest in the mangroves

waves create a natural habitat for fish, shrimp, crabs, and cowries. Each time the tide goes out, many people, young and old, flock to the mangrove forests to gather seashells and catch fish, shrimp, and crabs. The village of Qukou in Qiongshan County once contained 165 acres of mangrove forest, and the annual catch amounted to almost 20,000 pounds. However, during the "cultural revolution" the people were directed to reclaim the sea-bed and plant it with crops, so they chopped down the forests. As a result, there was no fresh water, the soil became very saline, no plants would grow, and the resources were exhausted because the seafood had lost its food supply and habitat.

The mangrove forest itself has considerable commercial value; it is known as "the iron crop of the sea." Some of the trees have hard wood with fine grain, bright color, and antirot properties, which makes them excellent for furniture, farm tools, and musical instruments. Common ceriops *(Ceriops tagal* C.B. Rab.*)*, stylose mangrove *(Rhizophora stylosa* Griff*)*, kandelia *(Kandelia candel* Druce*)*, and *Bruguiera gymnorhiza* produce excellent tanning materials. The fruits of *Rhizophora mucronata*, common sonneratia *(Sonneratia caseolaris* Engl.*)*, and shrub nipa *(Nipa fruticans* Wurmb.*)* are edible, and the juice from the stem of the shrub nipa flower can produce sugar, alcohol, and vinegar. The local farmers also use leaves from the mangrove trees as green fertilizer for their crops.

People have come to realize that in clearing away the mangrove forests with their unique ecosystems, they lost much more than they gained. Unfortunately, there wasn't such understanding when slogans like "Let the sea give way" and "We demand crops from the sea" prompted the wielding of hatchets. In those places where the mangrove trees had been chopped down, we saw no flowers, trees, songbirds, or fish. Instead we observed a lifeless, deserted beach. People there weren't able to profit from crops, aquatic resources, or the once-abundant firewood. Because of these bleak lessons, people are taking good care of the mangrove forests and are also

A bird-eye view of Dongzhaigang Nature Reserve

experimenting with artificial sowing to expand forestation. This is a very important activity not only because the mangrove forests are vital for the protection of fishing, agriculture, and a diversified economy, but also because biologically they are quite spectacular. Their trees demonstrate an adaptability to the environment that is startling and differs greatly from that of other plants in three important ways.

First, they have the very well developed root system I discussed earlier which provides nutrition and supports the trees firmly in the silt, even in times of strong winds and violent waves. The roots aboveground act as conduits so that buried roots will not suffocate from the silt's lack of oxygen.

Second, these trees are viviparous, producing seeds that germinate before becoming detached from the parent plant. This is common in many animals as well as in humans, and it is curious that the mangrove displays many of the physiological characteristics of the animal kingdom. Because the trees grow along the coast and are often washed by the tides and attacked by typhoons, the seeds do not have proper conditions to germinate separately. Instead, they develop buds and roots before leaving the mother tree, similar to a baby's development before leaving the womb. When conditions are right, the

seeds struggle into the mud with the force of their own weight, in a few hours rooting themselves securely so that the tidewater will not wash them away. If they *are* washed away, they float great distances to another spot, not dying even after two or three months in the water, because they have air pipes in their plumulose axes.

Walking in a mangrove forest, one can see many different kinds of seeds, some like pods, some like sheep horns, some like spindles, some like bullets. It is certainly unique in the plant kingdom to bear such a variety viviparously. This explains why the mangrove trees bloom and bear fruit throughout the year: New lives are constantly being born. The mangrove forest is truly an evergreen Great Wall.

There is yet another characteristic of this extraordinary ecosystem that is being studied to benefit man. To survive in the tides, the mangrove forests must have desalinating mechanisms. The trees are able to absorb the nutrition they require from the seawater and to discharge the extra salt by means of a desalinating system within their leaves. This is why some people term them "removers of seawater." At present, scientists are trying to discover the secret of the mangrove desalination process, planning to domesticate and cultivate trees that show extraordinary desalinating functions. Then they may grow wide belts of the special strain of trees between the east coast and the farmland, to desalinate the seawater and better irrigate the farmland there.

THE CRY OF ELD'S DEER

Early in the morning we climbed to the top of an observation tower, as tall as a four-story building, which had been built between a highway and a wire fence. The fence, more than six feet high, edges the highway for a great distance, encircling approximately 330 acres of tropical grassland. Among trees and dry shrubs live three herds of Hainan Eld's deer, about thirty in all. The fence protects the deer from hunters while preventing them from scattering, and allows tourists, many of whom come from far away, to see these rare animals.

The sky was cloudless, and because of our elevation we could see a great distance. We spotted the deer without difficulty even though they were outside the fence on the other side of the highway. A stag and three does were being chased by a black dog. Their graceful leaps back and forth through the green shrubbery were like a beautiful animated drawing. One of the reserve's workers told me: "They may be the herd that got out of

A herd of Eld's deer in flight

the enclosure when we had a general investigation last month. I saw them simply jump lightly over the fence to the other side." These deer never flee to the mountains or the forests, as they are too weak to defend themselves, yet they are able to survive because they run very fast and jump very far.

As these Eld's deer disappeared into the distant shrubbery, we caught sight of another herd inside the wire netting. A stag kept a distance of ten yards or so from four does who were peacefully eating grass. I was able to observe them carefully with binoculars. They looked similar to sikas, but did not have very distinct spots. However, a brown dorsal stripe embellished their two rows of white spots. Their coloration from back to belly to feet graduated from brown to yellow to white. Against the green grass they made a very pleasing picture. What attracted me most were the stag's beautiful antlers, both of which tilted slightly toward the front. These antlers help distinguish Eld's deer from other deer.

After descending the observation tower, we walked deeper into the bush along a small path. It had not rained in more than forty days, and the sun was extremely hot, beating down as if it were going to evaporate all the water in the ground. Many brooks and wells were dry, and most of the people had to carry water from great distances. Inside the wire enclosure, however, numerous deer clustered around four water holes. The area was very near the highway and a village, but the animals were reluctant to leave, possibly because of the availability of water. We eventually arrived at the spot where we had observed the deer.

Eld's deer have very keen vision and hearing; when we were still quite far away, they stretched their long necks and watched us vigilantly. Rather than run away, however, they uttered short cries, which set me thinking. Before I had left Beijing on this expedition, someone from the Ministry of Forestry had said to me: "There are two Eld's deer reserves on Hainan Island. One of them is good; the other is not. You should go to both, encouraging the people at the one that has done a good

Cyathea spinulosa, an ancient plant

job and criticizing those at the other, which has not done so well." After visiting both reserves, I found that even the better one had many deficiencies. Very few Hainan Eld's deer remained, and no one knew exactly what their fate would be. This bothered me greatly, and I began to feel great compassion for these creatures now that I had seen them and heard their cries.

People have many different opinions concerning the value of the Eld's deer. To scientists the deer belong to a subspecies found only on China's Hainan Island. Since they are few in number, it is extremely important to protect them from the imminent danger of extinction. They are valuable for scientific research, for the development of culture, education, and the economy, and for the production of medicine. The Chinese government has thus included them on the list of the most protected animals in China. The local people believe the deer can cure all sorts of diseases. They claim that after eating Eld's deer meat, one will be free from all disease and will not feel cold when swimming in the ocean. They also believe that the meat will help a woman suffering from infertility. They think, too, that the effects of this

so-called medicine are extremely long-lasting, with even the children and grandchildren of a person who has eaten the meat drawing benefits from it. All parts of the deer's body are considered rare treasures: the velvet antler covering, the fetus, the bones, the blood, the penis, the heart, the sinews, the skin, and the tail. More and more people desire these treasures, so the number of Eld's deer decreases daily, while the prices for parts of them increase rapidly. The more expensive the deer become, the more people want to hunt them; and the more they are hunted, the closer they move toward extinction.

There used to be many more Eld's deer on Hainan Island; decades ago they could be found among the shrubs, on the hillocks, and in the flatlands of Dongfang, Changjiang, Baisha, Ledong, Danxian, Qiongzhong, and Tunchang. However, after years of hunting them, coupled with destruction of their habitat, their distribution was reduced to only two places: the village of Bangxi in Baisha County and the village of Datian in the area of Dongfang. In 1975 the Guangdong government established reserves in those two places.

Because Bangxi had better natural conditions, it used to have more deer. However, the people there did not take the reserve seriously and ignored measures to protect it. The herd grew smaller and smaller until there were no deer left. In the village of Datian, however, the number of deer increased from twenty or so to more than seventy.

I visited the former reserve in Bangxi first, and the people working there took me on a tour. They pointed out the various grasses Eld's deer like to eat: *Lepisorus contortus* Ching, *Commelina diffuse, Commelina communis* and *Gossampinus malabaricus.* They also told me that the deer liked to hide themselves in *Locsa lateritia* Gill shrubs and that they often drank from the Zhubi River.

The total area of the sanctuary is only about 920 acres, and as more and more people arrived to live there, the land was parceled out and developed for planting. Conditions for the deer went from bad to worse. At the same time deer were killed in shocking numbers. Viewing the desolate areas in this reserve, I felt as if I were in a building where all the tenants had been evicted.

We then went to see the Datian reserve. After several days our main impression was that a lot of improvements had been made, but many problems remained.

The most significant achievement of this reserve was the annual increase in the numbers of deer. People who wish to observe Eld's deer will not be disappointed if they go to Datian. When buses from distant places pass through the reserve, drivers stop their vehicles for four or five minutes as soon as they see any deer in order to let passengers observe them.

One person, Wang Qian, former head of a protection station, deserves special praise. His accomplishments were noted in an article that appeared in the *South China Daily* under the headline AN ENTHUSIAST FOR PROTECTION OF ELD'S DEER. Born into an overseas Chinese family in Kampuchea, Wang returned to his motherland when it was liberated in 1949. After completing his academic studies, he took a job in a bank in Haikou City, Hainan Island. Accused of being a Rightist during the anti-Rightist Campaign, he was transferred to the Bureau of Forestry in Dongfang County, where he was in charge of forest-fire control and the overall protection of the forest. However, though he did his job well, he gave all his extra energy to protection of rare animals. After a thorough year-long investigation Wang knew quite well the circumstances of the Eld's deer. Hard study, long-term observation, and careful research made him a lay expert.

At that time hunting was very popular around Datian, so Wang had to work tirelessly to persuade the authorities and the local people of the importance of animal protection. Whenever a meeting was held in the county, he tried to have an item concerning the protection of Eld's deer placed on the agenda. Moreover, he designed and printed posters to put up in public places in the town and in the neighboring production brigades. He even went from door to door, into the fields, and onto construction sites, publicizing the significance of protecting the deer. Wherever hunting was permitted, Wang spoke with local authorities, townspeople, and the hunters themselves, enlightening them as to the jeopardy in which the Eld's deer were placed. Gradually, through his efforts, the region changed from one in which deer were hunted to one in which they were protected.

Some people gave the deer the same affection they gave their domestic animals. For example, a member of the Luowang Production Brigade saved a fawn from the mouth of a dog, then bought milk to feed it. Later, the fawn, carefully wrapped in a sheet, was transported to the protection station after a six-hour night journey in the mountains.

During the "cultural revolution," Wang Qian was transferred to a commune to become a statistician, but he maintained his devotion to deer protection. When he found that the number of Eld's deer was decreasing daily, he lost his appetite and began to sleep badly. He wrote to responsible members of the county government and earnestly requested that protective measures be taken to save this valuable natural heritage for the benefit of future generations.

In 1975, Wang was appointed head of the newly established protection station. Modestly learning from research scientists, such as Liu Zhenhe of the South China Rare Animal Institute, he completed difficult tasks day and night without complaint. Relying on the County Party Committee and uniting the local people, he led his staff and other workers in completing many basic construction projects, such as digging ditches, planting trees, building fences and firebreaks, and setting up watchtowers, and in putting up posters and organizing joint protection committees in the nearby communes. The Eld's deer increased from twenty-odd head to thirty, then fifty, then seventy, and on to eighty within seven or eight years.

THE GIBBON AND THE TROPICAL FOREST

My failure to see the gibbons on Hainan Island was a terrible disappointment. My itinerary was just too full, and since there are fewer than thirty gibbons there, it is very difficult to locate them.

The gibbon belongs to one of the four main groups of anthropoid apes and is the only anthropoid ape extant in China. Three species—the black-crested, the white-browed, and the white-handed—out of a total of seven in the world, have been recorded in China. The Hainan Island gibbon belongs to the black-crested species, since the female has a cluster of black hair on her head. Her body is yellow; the male's is black.

Like the chimpanzee, the gorilla, and the orangutan, the gibbon is closely related to *Homo sapiens*. Thus it provides valuable information in studying the evolution of anthropoid ape to man. In the past, gibbons occurred in great numbers throughout the tropical rain forests of Yunnan Province, the southern part of Guangxi Zhuang Autonomous Region, Hainan Island, and other southern localities. However, in recent years their numbers have been reduced greatly—to the point of extinction in some areas. In the early 1950's more than two thousand gibbons were living in the natural forests extending over nearly ten counties on Hainan Island, but before long they were on the brink of being wiped out as

Jianfengling Nature Reserve, Hainan Island

"Be careful."

trees were chopped down at random and the animals were caught and shot recklessly. In order to protect this rare animal, Bawangling Nature Reserve was established in 1980.

The remaining gibbons live in the forests and mountains there. Some gibbons previously discovered in the Jianfengling Nature Reserve south of the Bawangling Reserve have since disappeared. After visiting the mangrove and Eld's deer reserves, I went to these two reserves, and although I never saw a gibbon, I learned quite a lot about them and explored the tropical rain forest in which they live.

The small, long-armed, tailless gibbon can walk upright but uses that ability very little, as most of its life is spent in trees. Each family unit is headed by the father. The female undergoes a long gestation period, producing one litter in two or three years. A newborn gibbon has a hairless body with only a little fetal hair on top of its head. It can firmly grasp its mother's hair from the day of birth and will not fall off as the mother swings from tree to tree. A young gibbon stays with its family until it is seven or eight years old, when it reaches sexual maturity. Then it lives independently until it finds a mate.

Gibbons have a strong sense of territory and make only seasonal moves. If other groups invade their territory, a dispute develops. However, unlike other species of anthropoid apes and monkeys, they prefer verbal harassment to physical force. Their harangues commence with shouting from one side, followed by appropriate screeching from the other side. Then the two groups advance slowly to the territory's boundary, where the male gibbons confront each other, chasing, dodging, hanging from a branch by one arm, while the female gibbons screech as if to bolster their mates' morale. After about an hour the fighting stops and the two sides withdraw to their own areas.

Gibbons seem to like to shout, especially in the morning. The sound, starting low and slow, rising to high and fast, finally to shrill, can be heard for a mile or more in the forest. The gibbon does not have any way to protect itself from enemies. Unlike the macaque, which runs away as soon as it is even slightly alarmed, the gibbon opens its eyes wide to look around, not fleeing until it has appraised its enemy. Whenever a gibbon is attacked and knocked down, other gibbons come to rescue it. Even if one is shot dead, it will be snatched away by another one. This lack of defensive moves—or noble yet vulnerable behavior—may prove fatal to the gibbon and lead to its extinction.

Gibbons live only in tropical forests. If the temperature drops below 60 degrees Fahrenheit, the gibbons'

Four varieties of precious trees growing in twenty-one square feet of land

activity decreases; below 50 degrees, they shiver and huddle together for warmth. However, when the temperature is about 85 degrees and humans feel hot and uncomfortable, the gibbons are in their element.

The forests of the two reserves bear the distinct features of the gibbons' typical forest environment. I was impressed by the rich texture and complexity of the forest community. One spot in the forest is called "the seven-story building," because seven "stories" of vegetation grow with no intervening space. On one side of a mountain path I saw four different species of rare tall trees growing in only twenty square feet of earth. The biomass of the tropical forest can be as high as 94,600 pounds per *mu* (.1647 acre), more than in any other kind of forest or farmland. Moreover, the tropical forest is home to the greatest number of species.

In the two reserves, I found valuable trees such as *Hopea hainanensis, Homalium hainanensis, Madhuca hainanensis, Ormosia henryi, Bambusa textilis,* and *Dacrydium pierrei.* I also saw *Cephalotaxus hainanensis,* which contains medicinal properties first discovered in China as a cure for blood cancer, and *Cyathea spinulosa,* a relict plant that can be traced back to the prehistoric age of dinosaurs.

THE MACAQUES OF NANWAN

Traveling on the west side of Hainan Island, I visited five nature reserves that form a semicircle around the island. Our last stop was the Nanwan Nature Reserve to see the rhesus macaques. From Xincun harbor I took a ferry to Nanwanling—or Monkey Island, as it is called by the local people. From the ship I observed calm clear water and, to the south, Monkey Island with its luxuriant vegetation. In the east were distant mountains wrapped in mist. To the west, sailing vessels were scattered about on a sea the same rich hue as the sky. Back in the harbor I could see a forest of masts. The Aquatic Insti-

Nanwan Rhesus Macaque Nature Reserve is set up on this small island.

tute of the South Sea is near, and one can also see thousands of oyster shells in the pearl farms, where large brilliant pearls are cultured.

Monkey Island is connected to the mainland by only a flat, narrow strip of sand, making it an ideal reserve for the macaque.

The entire reserve, less than nine miles long and about one and a quarter miles wide, with a wedge-shaped sand dune in the middle, looks like a long bean floating on the sea. The classic novel *A Journey to the West* describes an island in the East Sea that is the kingdom of Aolai. This island also has a paradise for monkeys, called Huaguoshan (Fruit Hill). The Nanwan Reserve is a true Huaguoshan. Rugged rocks and caverns are found in the mountains. The climate is temperate, and more than 95 percent of the mountains is covered with dense vegetation. Except for trees planted by man at the foot of the mountains, vegetation is mainly tropical and secondary tropical bushes. Liana and herbaceous plants are also plentiful, and scattered trees can be noted in various locations. There are nearly a hundred species of plants as well as shrimp, prawns, crabs, and

Descending a tree

other shellfish which provide sufficient food for the macaques.

Taming the rhesus monkeys by giving them food begins at nine o'clock in the morning, when a keeper from the reserve station spreads mixed grains and dried sweet potatoes on a flat rock, then blows a whistle and shouts, "Come on! Come on!" Tourists hold their breath as they look toward the mountains. "Look! Look!" someone with keen eyes calls out. "There they are! Look at them!" The excitement builds as first the trees shake and then the monkeys can be seen swinging from limb to limb. All the trees on the mountain slope seem to be swaying and shaking. When the monkeys are close to the feeding rock, they stop, not daring to jump to the ground immediately. They even seem to be holding a brief meeting. Then a muscular male monkey, sitting on a branch higher than the others and watching the entire scene with a glare like a tiger eyeing its prey, appears to give a signal to the other monkeys, and one after the other they climb down from the trees.

A female clutching a baby around the waist snatches a piece of dried sweet potato with lightning speed, races back up the tree, and pops the sweet potato into her child's mouth. Other monkeys follow, some not even running away afterward. The male monkey, sitting motionless at the top of the tree, seems to bear a heavy responsibility for protecting the other monkeys. The keeper throwing food to them says that this monkey is their king. The others all obey him.

Cautiously approaching the feeding spot, some tourists throw candy, bananas, and peanuts to the monkeys. The monkeys quickly snatch the food and put it into their mouths. Obviously, they are used to strangers. Although five or six cameras are clicking in front of them, they don't leave. The tourists are equally unwilling to go.

Wang Yixiang, a responsible worker at the reserve,

Hearing the whistle, the monkeys come in droves.

gave me a detailed introduction. Two groups of macaques had already been tamed, and the staff was just beginning to work with a third group. The training began in 1974. Autumn and winter are the best seasons, because there is little food available in the wild and the monkeys are in a state of semistarvation. The feeding spots are places where the monkeys usually go. Every day at a fixed time food is put out, and the monkeys go to eat regularly. After a month or so the keeper appears before the monkeys, trying not to frighten them. When they become accustomed to him, he appears more openly, blowing his whistle and shouting, "Come on! Come on!" before feeding time. The monkeys gradually connect man and his shouting with eating, and eventually begin moving to the feeding spot as soon as they hear the whistle. The feeding spot can then be moved step by step down the mountain to a more convenient location.

The keeper can also move a few feet closer to the spot each day, walking slowly and deliberately. When the keeper is very close, no monkey dares to take the food, even though they have left the trees. The monkey king, menacing eyes glaring at the keeper, seems to speculate about what all this means. The keeper must remain cool and calm, sitting to one side as if nothing is happening. This deadlock is broken only by the monkeys' eagerness to eat. One or two suddenly run to the food and flee instantly with a good handful. When others see nothing terrible has happened to them, they follow suit. After a while the monkeys develop enough courage not only to grab food from the hands of the keeper but to walk up to strangers.

The macaques are tamed not just to please tourists but also so that scientists may better observe their ecology and social structure. This is extremely important for the monkeys' protection, for the study of their breeding habits, and for the utilization of wild species. Through observation, recording, and analysis over the past few years, much information about these two monkey groups has been gathered.

The monkeys range one to three miles outside the reserve, although some go longer distances, including climbing several mountains. The Nanwan macaques usually go no more than 1,000 to 1,600 feet, though one group was recorded at 2,600 feet. The monkeys occupy two or three mountaintops, especially the tamed "east group" and "west group," whose behavior is rather evident. The border between them is a ditch about 650 feet long. The two groups rarely cross the border or fight with each other. However, the scattered male monkeys have a wider scope of activity, including three to five other mountains. When the females are in heat, from late autumn to early winter, the scattered males search the monkey groups, trying to find an opportunity to mate with a female monkey. Unfortunately, they are often chased away by either the leader of the group or the other monkeys. The range of activity for groups within the reserve is limited by the size of the region and the food supply. The density of monkeys is quite high.

A group usually includes old, middle-aged, and young monkeys, led by a strong male. Groups with many females may have two or more leaders who command and control the other monkeys. The leader is responsible for their protection, mediates their quarrels, and freely selects a female as his mate. The other monkeys must obey his commands. Fertility for the females begins toward the end of October. During this time many potential mates are attracted, and a kind of power play takes place among the leaders. The monkeys chase one another up the trees, often tumbling back to earth. They snap at one another, biting off ears and nipping toes and noses until their bodies are covered with wounds. When they recover from their injuries, they continue to fight. After repeated trials of strength the defeated monkeys are either forced to leave the group and lead a solitary life or are allowed to remain in the group in a subservient position, acknowledging the winner in battle as king and obeying submissively. The king of the west group has changed three times in the past several years. The first king had a cut on his mouth, the second on his nose. These cuts are emblems of glory for the winners. The third king has no wound, showing he was stronger than his opponents. These monkeys follow a eugenic law of fighting among males to strengthen the group.

All adult females have menstrual periods and come into heat from late October to early February. December and January are peak months of fertility, and pregnancy lasts six months, so births occur mainly in June. The monkeys give birth every year or twice in three years, always to only one offspring. According to statistics, the average annual growth rate of a group is approximately 25 percent, with the male rate higher than the female. When the male reaches maturity, he is usually expelled from the group, so the number of males in a particular group tends to remain constant. This suggests two measures that could be taken. First, a few male monkeys between the ages of one and three could be caught for observation by the scientific research unit. Income from selling the monkeys could be used for improving the environment for development of the species groups. Second, scientific research into why there are more male monkeys than female monkeys should be accelerated, enabling appropriate measures to be taken to increase the proportion of females.

With the assistance of the scientific research unit, the staff of the reserve has begun painting numbers on the faces of the tamed monkeys. Already thirty-one monkeys from the east group and twenty-one from the west group have been numbered. The number identification of monkeys facilitates the gathering of more precise data on the unity, division, separation, and mating practices of the groups.

The macaque belongs to the second class of animals under state protection. These monkeys have made considerable contribution to scientific experimentation, medicine, and space flight, and have provided insights into the cultural life of early man.

THE YANGTZE ALLIGATOR MIRACULOUSLY SAVED FROM EXTINCTION

Just after attending a symposium on mammals, the group I was with left Hefei to visit the Xuancheng breeding farm of the Yangtze alligator, an imperiled creature that can now be saved from the verge of extinction.

238 LITTLE ALLIGATORS

In an unobtrusive, ordinary village house, looking somewhat like a greenhouse with a glass roof over its four brick walls, a fire was burning in the stove and an electric heater was on. The sunshine, the fire in the stove, and the electric heater all combined to warm the room to a temperature of 86 degrees Fahrenheit. The aquarium, half sand, half water, held more than two hundred squirming little alligators. They looked a bit like the Chinese crocodile lizards *(Shinisaurus crocodilurus)*, found in the Yao Mountains in Guangxi Zhuang Autonomous Region, and also like little geckos. Some were whisking their big tails, as long as their bodies; some were stretching their necks, turning up their noses, and looking left and right; but most were just lying motionless on top of each other. When the keepers threw little fish to them, they all came to life. They would toss a fish to and fro ten to twenty times, until they could get it in the right position to swallow all at once. When two little alligators got hold of the same little fish, neither would give in. If one alligator flung the other one down, it would not loosen its hold on the fish but would turn over, gather its strength, and fling the other alligator down in turn. They went on like this until they had torn the fish in two; then each swallowed its booty.

We paused for a long time in front of the aquarium in admiration of an important scientific achievement. Because the Yangtze alligator was on the verge of extinction, these 238 little lives represented a quite significant number: half as many as exist in the wild.

THE DRAGON AND THE DINOSAUR

The dragon is a legendary animal that does not really exist, and the dinosaur is a once-existing animal that has long been extinct. Are they in any way related to the crocodilians? Yes, indeed. In tracing the long history of the crocodilians, one must mention both the dragon and the dinosaur, as myth and legend are often the shadows of reality.

Some scientists claim that the dragon is actually the incarnation of the crocodile. In ancient China two species of crocodilians thrived: the Yangtze alligator and the saltwater crocodile *(Crocodylus porosus)*. In ancient books the saltwater crocodile was also called "flood dragon"; and the alligator, "swine woman's dragon." The local people now, in fact, generally call the alligator "earth dragon." The *Zuozhuan (Zuo Qiuming's commentary on the Spring and Autumn Annals—722–484* B.C.*)* records people "keeping dragons," saying that in the days of Huangdi, the Yellow Emperor, and Shun (two legendary Chinese monarchs, said to have lived sometime between about the twenty-sixth century B.C. and the twenty-second century B.C.), there were specialists qualified to keep dragons and an official in charge of keeping them. At that time, breeding dragons was regarded as a specialized skill. From this we may conclude that the "dragon" was not a purely imaginary animal but one that really existed.

But what kind of animal was it? Let us compare the dragon and the crocodile: enormous mouth, two rows of huge teeth, clearly marked scales, four feet, a long tail, and the ability to live both on land and in water. Their characteristics are identical. In ancient times most tribes of the Central Plains (the region comprising the middle and lower reaches of the Yellow River) took amphibians or fish as their totems, so naturally the crocodile became an object of worship. As the crocodile gradually became almost extinct in the Central Plains, all sorts of tales were spun around it, and as the rulers deified the animal, the dragon became a miraculous and mysterious creature.

Thus there seems to be ample reason to say the dragon originated from the crocodile rather than from the serpent or any other animal. Of course, the history of the crocodilians can best be illustrated by the crocodilians themselves. From archeological findings we know that in the past they existed in greater number and variety and were much more widely distributed in this part of the country. Archeologists have so far discovered seventeen genera of crocodilian fossils in China. Along with the twenty-five species that still exist in the world today, these fossils furnish important data for the study of the evolution of animals and nature.

As for the history of the crocodilians, we have to trace back to the time of the dinosaur. Paleontologists hold that crocodilians have the same pedigree as the ancestors of the different species of dinosaurs that emerged during the early Mesozoic Era—the thecodonts. Therefore they are the only existing relict species of this line of descent and may well be called living fossils. In fact, they are better qualified for that title than either the giant panda or the Chinese river dolphin. During the past 200 million years innumerable species and genera of animals have come and gone in this universe, including the different species of dinosaur that disappeared 70 million years ago, but the crocodilians have met the challenge of nature and lived on staunchly to this day. Fossils show that during the tens of millions of years that passed between the protosaurs and modern crocodilians, their structure changed hardly at all. Thus the skin, teeth, and skeleton of the present-day crocodilians have some characteristics similar to those of the dinosaur. Some scientists have used the crocodile as a model in reconstituting the appearance of certain species of dinosaurs.

THE SALTWATER CROCODILE AND THE YANGTZE ALLIGATOR

In the view of scientists, these very ancient and precious animals have great scientific value and are in urgent need of protection.

As long as 1,100 years ago the eminent writer Han Yu (768–824) of the Tang Dynasty, who was at the time prefectural governor of Chaozhou, wrote an essay entitled "Funeral Oration to the Crocodile" which achieved great popularity. Leaving aside the social implications of the essay and focusing on the crocodile, we find the essay tells us that during Han Yu's time a species of large, man-eating crocodile was so numerous in the region it endangered the lives and property of the people; and the people had such fear of them that the prefectural governor issued an "ultimatum," warning the crocodiles to move away within a limited period of

A Yangtze alligator and its natural habitat

The breeding ponds at the Yangtze Alligator Breeding and Research Center

time or he would order people equipped with powerful bows and poisonous arrows to kill all of them. Then, during the Song Dynasty (960–1279), when the vice-minister Xia Yuanji went to Chaozhou, it is reported that people threw quicklime into the sea to poison and kill the crocodiles.

Because people had such a deep aversion to crocodiles and got into the habit of killing them, and because the climate in the coastal areas of the country changed, this saltwater animal struggled on until the end of the Ming Dynasty (1368–1644) and finally became extinct. Only a distant relative, the comparatively small, freshwater Yangtze alligator, remained, and this animal is also now in imminent danger of dying out.

According to records, the Yangtze alligator abounded in the regions of Jiujiang, Hankou, Anqing, Wuhu, Dangtu, Zhenjiang, Suzhou, and Shanghai, but a survey made between 1951 and 1956 by Zhu Chengguan showed its distribution to be much more restricted. It could be found only in river valleys and in the vicinity of the Yangtze River tributaries in Anhui Province; in Zhejiang and Jiangsu provinces it had become almost extinct. Recently another survey in Anhui Province showed that distribution had again been reduced. In places such as Dangtu, Wuhu, and Fanchang, where Zhu Chengguan had recorded considerable numbers of alligators, they had become extinct, while in other regions their numbers had fallen drastically. According to a general survey, China has fewer than five hundred Yangtze alligators.

The imminent danger to the Yangtze alligator stems mainly from large-scale conversion of wasteland for cultivation and construction of irrigation works, seriously damaging the alligator's habitat. Reckless killing and capturing also threaten the species. Although the Yangtze alligator does not harm people, it does harass the fish and domestic fowl bred by the peasants; it burrows and lives in holes, often doing much damage to the dikes and embankments; and as it goes out on its nocturnal pursuits, it often ravages the crops. The people of the region regard it as a pest; they beat any they come across, smash their eggs, and destroy their nests. Especially in times of serious flood or drought, when alligators can no longer stay in their holes and have to go out by day to look for food, they are slain in great numbers. In some regions people use sodium pentachlorophenate to poison and kill the oncomelania, a type of snail the Yangtze alligator eats, thus exposing it to secondary poisoning.

So today the Yangtze alligator is facing the same fate as the saltwater crocodile.

THREE ACHIEVEMENTS IN THREE YEARS

In order to save the Yangtze alligator from extinction, two measures have been taken in Anhui Province. A nature reserve has been established in the five counties—Xuancheng, Langxi, Guangde, Jingxian, and Nanling—where the alligator has survived. Protection of the alligators is assigned to a particular lumber camp, production brigade, or individual in the region where the animal is found. Those who protect the alligators are rewarded, while those who harm them are punished. If alligators ravage crops, the state compensates farmers. The second measure is a breeding farm that has been set up in Xuancheng County, where the Yangtze alligator is found in relatively concentrated numbers. On the farm the workers experiment with artificial breeding.

Because the Yangtze alligator is of a very particular disposition and because in the past little attention was paid to observing and studying the animal, artificial breeding poses many difficulties. Zoos in the country keep one hundred or so alligators, but in the past none of those alligators laid any eggs, so artificial breeding and incubation were out of the question. The breeding farm appointed Chen Bihui, associate professor in the department of biology at Anhui Normal University, as instructor and gave him a free hand in directing all

Artificially bred alligators

One-year-old artificially bred alligators

A young alligator gets a health check.

scientific and technological matters. Whenever there was any problem, he was consulted and his advice followed explicitly. Chen Bihui is a sincere, amiable, middle-aged intellectual who gets on extremely well with everyone at the breeding farm. He has been studying the Yangtze alligator for more than twenty years and in 1976 experimented with artificial breeding of the alligator in his laboratory. With Chen Bihui's leadership, the farm's work has proceeded fairly smoothly, and in three years' time it solved three problems.

In 1981 it solved the problem of artificial incubation. During the first year of experimentation very few alligators were hatched. The scientists summed up their experiences and found three essentials had to be observed during the period of incubation: The temperature should be kept between 82 and 86 degrees Fahrenheit; the relative humidity should be kept above 90 percent; and attention should be paid to the supply of oxygen during the final period of incubation. The reward of determin-

ing these three critical factors was the hatching of more than thirty little alligators.

One can imagine how happy the scientists were! But not for long, for the little alligators all went on a hunger strike. Their keepers did not know what or how to feed them, so they extracted the meat of snails with a bamboo pin and pushed it into the little alligators' mouths or used a syringe to inject eggs down their throats. Who would have thought that these delicate wild animals would not thrive on such generous human treatment! Some died of infarction, some starved to death, and some died of injuries sustained when their throats were pierced. On top of all that, the indoor temperature was not high enough, so the little alligators did not like to move and the protein food blocked their stomachs and could not be digested, causing decomposition of the food followed by illness and death. Even those that barely managed to live on could not survive hibernation for lack of nutrition. Finally, they all died.

The scientists did not lose heart, however. In 1982 they solved the problem of rearing the little alligators. Again they summed up their experiences over the past year and the lessons to be learned, further improved the rate of incubation, and hatched 143 alligators. This time they changed their rearing methods mainly by training

Laying eggs

Hunting for a meal

the young reptiles in every way possible to catch their own food. In a hothouse temperature of over 86 degrees Fahrenheit, the keepers were sweating away, stripped to the waist, trying to tempt the alligators with bait as if they were fishing. At first the little alligators did not know what it was all about and remained indifferent. But as time went on, these moving pieces of food tickled their instincts or appetites and they snapped at the tiny fish. That was it! They had all of a sudden crossed the threshold of life and would look after themselves. That year, 87 of the hatchlings survived. When we saw this group in a small pond, they were already about a foot long and thirteen months old.

In 1983 the scientists solved the problem of getting the artificially bred alligators to lay eggs. The Yangtze alligators in zoos had never laid any eggs, nor had those at the breeding farm. Why?

The first breeding farm covered an area of only about one *mu*—less than one fifth of an acre. The more than fifty Yangtze alligators were squeezed together, so everybody called it the alligators' prison. To release them from prison, the entire staff of the breeding farm worked hard one winter and constructed a twenty-five-*mu* farm— more than four acres—reproducing the natural environment of the Yangtze alligator. Sure enough, for the first time twelve female alligators laid 220 eggs. From these, 130 were selected for artificial incubation. That year more than 200 alligators were hatched, both "wild" and "domestic" ones. Meanwhile the alligators in the "prison" did not produce a single egg, and even on the big breeding farm only a minority among the female alligators laid eggs, and these were often ravaged by the other alligators. So another large-scale breeding farm was started, 1,420 times the size of the "prison." The scientists' success had attracted much attention from various circles. To help them build this new farm, the provincial Forestry Department allocated 160,000 yuan and the Ministry of Forestry 1 million yuan. The breeding farm has already been officially named the Yangtze Alligator Breeding Research Center.

Professor Chen came specially from the university to accompany us during our visit to the various facilities of the breeding farm. We were also accompanied by leading staff members. It took us a full two hours to tour the site. Our hosts were obviously pleased as they showed us around. "This is the reservoir. This is the bamboo forest. This is the chestnut garden and that the grassland. If you come again in a few years, you will see not only many more Yangtze alligators but all kinds of wild animals running about the grounds, all kinds of wild birds flying in the sky, and all sorts of fish and crustaceans swimming in the water. A new ecological system will emerge here: Birds will feed on destructive insects, thus protecting the vegetation; the vegetation will feed the herbivores, and the excrement of the animals will breed fish—and fish are what the Yangtze alligator lives on."

An even bigger project was in the works—expansion of the breeding farm from 234 acres to 8,235 acres, including 116 reservoirs. The Ministry of Forestry had set the goal of two thousand Yangtze alligators by 1990. Now it seemed they might reach this goal ahead of time. If the number of Yangtze alligators could be increased very rapidly, part would be used to supply zoos, museums, and scientific research institutes in the country;

part would be returned to nature; and another part could be used as raw material for the leather, pharmaceutical, and food industries. Our hosts told us a great deal more, but as we were walking all the time, I could not take down much of what they said.

Although they had been successful, they realized that breeding Yangtze alligators was not like breeding pigs or chickens. Even breeding pigs, one may have to deal with swine erysipelas, and breeding chickens, with chicken pest. The Yangtze alligator had just started to live among people after having lived in the wild for 200 million years. How could one expect that there would be no more difficulties or unforeseen situations?

NATURE IS THE BEST TEACHER

After visiting the breeding farm, I kept wondering why it was that the zoos, with their extensive experience in the artificial reproduction of animals, had not made much progress with the alligator after studying the animal for more than ten years, while the breeding farm had been successful as soon as scientists had taken a hand in it.

It is not an easy question to answer. I have known Chen Bihui ever since we met at the inauguration of the Chinese Mammalogy Society in Dalian, and we have become old friends. Although this scientific achievement has not yet been publicized, he did not keep anything from me, apart from his personal contribution to it. I seized every opportunity to find the answer to my question, not going straight to the point, but asking one question after another.

QUESTION: *How did you know that the temperature during incubation had to be kept between eighty-two and eighty-six degrees Fahrenheit?*
ANSWER: From our observations in the field. The Yangtze alligator hatches its eggs in the hottest season in this

region. We noticed that the alligator covered its eggs with grass and weeds, which had a fermenting and heating effect. From foreign reference material and our own observations we discovered that the Yangtze alligator has a peculiar characteristic. The sex of human beings and of the greatest number of animals is decided by the difference in sex chromosomes, but the sex of the Yangtze alligator is acquired and is determined primarily by the temperature during incubation. If the temperature tends to be on the high side, it will produce male alligators; if it is on the low side, it will produce females. We find alligators' nests everywhere, on northern and southern slopes, on sunny and shady sides. These different climatic conditions naturally adjust the proportion of male to female alligators.

QUESTION: *How did you know about the humidity levels?*

ANSWER: From observation in the field. You just have to note the humid weather here in July and August and observe that the alligators' nests are near the water, and everything explains itself. We also noticed that the female alligators went back and forth from their nests to the water all the time, thus wetting their nests with the water from their bodies. From this we learned that the alligators require a high level of humidity during hatching time. Also, alligators' eggs have a much thicker consistency than birds' eggs, so if the mothers do not take care, their eggs may evaporate or spoil . . . .

QUESTION: *How did you think of supplying them with oxygen?*

ANSWER: Again, from observations made in the field. During the final period of incubation we often saw the parent alligators turning the grass in their nests over. It is their natural behavior but has the effect of airing the nest and supplying oxygen. Then, if we look into the physiology of incubation, we see that by this time the lungs of the little alligators will have developed fully and started their breathing function. If oxygen is lacking, they are likely to suffocate in their eggs.

QUESTION: *How did you think of training the little alligators to catch their food?*

Newborn Yangtze alligators

ANSWER: From observations in the field, too. Catching food is the first lesson carnivorous animals have to learn to be able to live independently. Female alligators cannot possibly rear their young by using bamboo pins or syringes. When we failed at first, we had to think of how the female alligator trains its young.

QUESTION: *How did you figure out what would make the Yangtze alligator lay eggs?*

ANSWER: Again this is the result of our field observation. The Yangtze alligator mostly moves about individually, its diet is fairly varied, it needs to hibernate, and it requires a quiet environment to mate and lay its eggs. All these factors combined contribute to the alligator's laying eggs. In zoos these conditions can hardly be realized, and the "prison," too, lacks such conditions, so the alligators do not lay any eggs there. We began to pay attention to all these factors and built a breeding farm with caves for hibernation, all sorts of food, and restrictions on visitors during the reproductive season. Soon the alligators started laying eggs.

By now I understood. The scientists had had the best, most reliable and most authoritative teacher—nature.

Although all living creatures are complex, of different shapes and colors, they are not unpredictable or incoherent. All living things have their own pattern. The task of the scientist is to diagnose those patterns accurately. Whenever scientists confront problems, they ask nature, and nature is sure ultimately to give them the answer. Nature is just and unselfish; she does not withhold secrets from anyone; but she is strict and demanding with her students. In order to study the Yangtze alligator, Chen Bihui traveled all over southern Anhui Province. He went to the most remote, sparsely populated, and inaccessible places as long as there was something to be learned about the Yangtze alligator. To study the cave life of the alligator, he dug out scores of caves, the deepest of which was almost a hundred feet in length and took more than twenty days to dig. The Yangtze alligator is mainly active at night, so Chen would take his flashlight and roam about the deserted banks and wastelands night after night, observing the alligator to see how it hunted for food, looked for a mate, then mated, and brooded. In the pitch-dark night he could distinguish, at a distance of sixty-five to one hundred feet, a glowworm from the glitter of an alligator's eye. He got so familiar with the alligator's cry that he could distinguish five different sounds: courtship, refusal to mate, anger, fright, and reaction to low atmospheric pressure.

Through layers of questions I had come to the core of the matter, so I finally asked, "Others have worked on the project for over ten years, without result. How is it that you succeeded in just three years?"

I expected him to follow my trend of thought and answer accordingly, but he said only, "My work is a little more stupid than people usually imagine."

The answer came as a surprise, yet sounded familiar. It was not the first time I had heard something like it. It reminded me of Zhong Jixin, who discovered the *Cathaya argyrophylla* at Huaping; of Hu Jinchu, who searched the bamboo groves for panda feces; of Liu Yinzeng, who traversed the green hills far and wide and finally found the crested ibis; of Zhang Zhen, who caught serpents and planted medicinal herbs in the Wuyi Mountains; of Wang Qian and Liu Zhenhe, who worried over the fate of the Eld's deer. I had met all of them and knew their achievements. Whenever I thought of them, it was always with great respect, sympathy, and high esteem for their complete dedication to their cause. Perhaps their success was due to the development of a single idea or to a rare opportunity, but behind it was an enormous amount of sustained, tedious, ordinary, and even "stupid" labor. All of them are good students of nature, and nature has not let them down, favoring each of them with a golden key to unlock her mysteries.

A
GENERAL
SURVEY
OF
CHINA'S
NATURE
RESERVES

China is a vast and diverse country. Its 3,400 miles from north to south cross five different climatic zones: cold-temperate, intermediate-temperate, warm-temperate, subtropical, and tropical. Its 3,200 miles from east to west pass through humid, semihumid, semiarid, and arid zones strongly influenced by monsoons. Over time and with the movement of the earth, various landforms have evolved, from Mount Qomolangma, 29,028 feet above sea level, the highest peak in the world, to Aiding Lake, 505 feet below sea level, the second-lowest lake in the world. Such an extent and such extremes provide a superb natural setting for abundant varieties of wildlife.

China's 30,000 varieties of higher plants make up 10 percent of the world's varieties. Many have survived from ancient times and range from arctic to tropical flora. Little affected by temperatures of the Quaternary Ice Age, many varieties long extinct elsewhere in the Northern Hemisphere can still be found in China.

About two hundred genera of plants are special to China. Camellia *(Camellia chrysotha)*, Chinese golden larch *(Pseudolarix amabilis)*, and the dove tree *(Davidia involucrata)* are well known in the world. Many plants of the gurjun family *(Dipterocarpaceae)* and other precious plants also grow in the tropical rain forest, such as the Chinese parashorea *(Parashorea chinensis)*, almost two hundred feet high, Hainan hopea *(Hopea hainanensis)*, which will not rot for dozens of years underground; greytwig *(Schoepfia schreb)*, which cannot be damaged by moths and water; and Hainan plum-yew *(Cephalotaxus hainanensis)*, a source of medicine used in the treatment of cancer. There are many original varieties of cultivated plants in China. Wild rice, wild tea tree, wild litchi, wild walnut, wild apple, wild chestnut, and wild cucumber are the genetic sources for breeding and improving seeds. Other plants are sources of medicine, vegetable fat, starch, fiber, and spice. Many ancient trees still grow in all parts of the country. The metasequoia No. 1 in Lichuan, Hubei Province; David keteleeria *(Keteleeria davidiana)* in Shennongjia; the ginkgo *(Ginkgo*

Zhangjiajie National Forest Park in Hunan Province

China has 4,400 species of vertebrates, representing 10 percent of the world's vertebrates. Among them there are 450 species of land animals, 1,186 of birds, 196 of amphibians, 320 of reptiles, and 2,000 of aquatic animals. Many, such as the giant panda, the golden monkey, the takin, the white-lipped deer, the brown-eared pheasant, the Chinese river dolphin *(Lipotes vexillifer)*, and the Chinese alligator are special to China. China has 9 of the 15 species of cranes in the world and 56 of the 276 species of pheasant, 19 of which are found only in China.

China's nature reserves can be divided into four basic types.

1. RESERVES TO PROTECT NATURAL ECOSYS-TEMS. Reserves for natural ecosystems, particularly forest ecosystems, were among the first to be established in China and are now the largest and most numerous of China's nature reserves. Huzhong Nature Reserve in the northeast, where the Greater Hinggang Mountains and Yilehuli Mountains meet in Heilongjiang Province, lies between 2,300 and 3,300 feet above sea level and covers some 480,000 acres. The annual mean temperature is 21 degrees Fahrenheit, and temperatures can fall as low as 62 degrees below zero during the eight-month winter in the region. The area belongs to the frozen-earth growing zone, and because of poor drainage, low temperature, and low fertility of the soil, the sparse trees are deformed and sickly. Even trees over two centuries old are no more than four inches in diameter. Closely related to the permafrost are primitive marshes that provide valuable material for the study of wetland succession, and supply large quantities of peat, natural fiber, and forage. The reserve contains moose, red deer, lynx *(Felis lynx)*, snow hare, and brown bear *(Ursus arctos)*, and coldwater fish, including *Prachmystax lenur* and *Hucho tajmen*.

Changbai Mountain Nature Reserve in Jilin Province

biloba) in Tanzhe Temple near Beijing are precious living fossils.

China's fauna extend over two large biogeographic regions: the Palaearctic northern and the eastern ocean area. China and Mexico are the only countries that include both regions. Moose *(Alces alces)* and snow hare *(Lepus timidus)* inhabit the cold-temperate zone; Manchurian tiger and sable *(Martes zibellina)* the temperate zone; white-lipped deer *(Cervus albirostris)* the Qinghai-Tibet Plateau; giant panda, golden monkey, and Chinese alligator *(Alligator sinensis)* the subtropical zone; and wild elephants, gibbon, gaur *(Bibos gaurus)*, and hornbill the southern subtropical and tropical zones.

White-headed langur (*Presbytis leucocephalus*)

Red-crowned crane (*Grus japonensis*) in Zhalong Nature Reserve

Hanas Nature Reserve in the Altai Range in Xinjiang Uygur Autonomous Region, close to the Soviet Union, contains China's most important active glaciers, as well as valuable examples of Siberian flora and fauna. Found there are Korean pine, fir, larch, and dragon spruce; argali sheep *(Ovis ammon)*, ibex *(Capra ibex)*, capercaillie *(Tetrao spp)*, hazel grouse *(Tetrastes bonasia)*, snow hare, and black grouse *(Lyrurus tetrix)*.

Changbai Range Nature Reserve, which covers an area of approximately 470,000 acres on the border of Jilin Province and North Korea, is a typical intermediate-temperate zone forest ecosystem. The main peak, Baitou Mountain, rising 9,000 feet above sea level, is the highest peak in northern Eurasia. The reserve is rich in plant resources, including 213 varieties of lichen, 170 varieties of moss, 127 varieties of brake, 17 varieties of gymnosperm, and 1,460 varieties of angiosperm. There are ancient plants that date back to the Tertiary Period, varieties of European and Siberian plants, elements of Korean and Japanese flora, polar plants carried south by glacier movements and left on the frozen mountain plateaus, and in the warmer valleys subtropical plants similar to those found in the southeastern part of China. Together, these create the rich and unique flora of the Changbai Range. From the deep ravines to the main peaks can be found vegetation of every climatic zone from temperate to frigid; needleleaf and broadleaf mixed forest, needleleaf forest, Ermans birch forest, and mountain tundra. This well-preserved ecosystem has long been the subject of scientific research and is an important base for the study of ecology, geography, climatology, and animal and plant life.

The Taibai Mountain Nature Reserve is located in the Qinling Range, which separates the Yellow River Valley from the Yangtze River Valley and divides China into southern and northern parts. The reserve covers an area of 133,864 acres and from south to north displays a marked transition in climatic conditions and ecological composition. It contains 1,700 identified varieties of seed plants, many of which are peculiar to the region and

Shuzeng Waterfall in Jinzhaigon Nature Reserve in Sichuan Province

under state protection. These include *Larix chinensis, Cercidiphyllum japonicum, Tetracentron sinense,* and *Dipteronia sinensis.* Fauna special to the region include giant panda, golden monkey, takin, crested ibis, and black ibis.

Besides the nature reserves created to protect forest ecosystems, there are reserves to protect marine, island, lake, pastureland, marsh, and desert ecosystems.

2. RESERVES TO PROTECT PRECIOUS ANIMALS. The giant panda has long been famous throughout the world. It is estimated that about a thousand of these protected animals are distributed throughout the mountainous region on the borders of Shaanxi, Gansu, and Sichuan provinces, with most of them in Sichuan Province. Since 1963, ten nature reserves have been established in the regions frequented by giant pandas, eight in Sichuan, one in Shaanxi, and one in Gansu. Wolong Nature Reserve in Sichuan, built in 1975, is the largest and best known of these.

Compared with countries at the same latitude, China is rich in species of apes and monkeys, though it has fewer than countries nearer the equator. There are slender loris, three species of gibbon, and species special to China such as the white-headed langur, golden monkey, Yunnan golden monkey, Guizhou golden monkey, and

Taiwan monkey. The rhesus monkey, numerically the largest species in China, can be found as far north as the mountains in the northeastern part of Hebei Province—farther north than anywhere else in the world. Many nature reserves have been set up to preserve these precious apes and monkeys.

At present China has 1,186 species of birds, 13 percent of the world's total. Many of them are rare species and 73 of them are currently under state protection. These precious birds are protected in special reserves located at their breeding and wintering grounds, as well as at places where they rest during migration.

3. RESERVES TO PROTECT FOREST VEGETATION AND PRECIOUS PLANTS. The Fenglin Nature Reserve, created in 1958, and the Liangshui Nature Reserve, created in 1980, in the Lesser Hinggang Mountains in Heilongjiang Province are two important bases for the protection and development of varieties of Korean pine. The Korean pine is a relict plant ideal for use in the building, mining, and communications industries.

The Baiyinaobao Nature Reserve, created in 1979 in the eastern part of the Yangshandake Desert in Inner Mongolia, preserves an area of 14,826 acres of virgin Meyer spruce forest *(Picea meyerii)*—a rarity in a semiarid prairie. The forest is an oasis in the desert and plays a vital part in preventing the land from being swallowed up by sand. It also provides grass for domestic animals and raw materials for the building and fiber industries. This is an important base for the study of the growth, development, and ecology of forests of this type and provides valuable scientific information necessary for the creation of new artificial forests in semiarid regions.

4. NATURE RESERVES FOR OTHER SPECIAL PURPOSES. Special reserves have been created to protect areas with valuable geological features, such as

A. Shanwang Nature Reserve in Shandong Province

B. Tianchi Lake in the crater of an extinct volcano in Changbai Nature Reserve in Jilin Province

C. Hanasi Lake Nature Reserve in Xingjiang Uygur Autonomous Region

glacial sites, karst formations, and hot springs, as well as fossil-rich areas important in the study of natural history.

Wudalianchi (five-linked-lakes) Nature Reserve, established in 1980, covers 172,970 acres. This is a natural museum of live volcanoes. Two out of the fourteen volcanoes erupted between 1719 and 1721, the last eruption cutting Bailong River into five linked lakes. This created a beautiful scenic spot with valuable mineral resources, as well as hot springs that possess medicinal value.

Shanwang in Linxun County, Shandong Province, is a nature reserve created mainly to preserve an area rich in fossils.

Diaoshuilou Waterfall in Jingpo Lake Nature Reserve in Heilongjiang Province

Natural parks such as Huangshan and Lushan are another kind of nature reserve. Their natural beauty provides an ideal habitat for precious animals and attracts tourists from all over the world.

Other nature reserves are being set up near cities, factories, and mines. Nature reserves have been created in Lingshan, Baihuashan, Songshan, and Wulingshan around Beijing in accordance with overall construction plans for the capital. These reserves directly or indirectly affect the city ecosystem and contribute much to the improvement of city life.

Qianshan Nature Reserve has been established six miles from Anshan, China's largest iron and steel works. Its forests cover an area of seventeen square miles and are estimated to consume 4,400 tons of carbon dioxide and exude 3,000 tons of oxygen per day. Qianshan

Yandangshan Nature Reserve in Zhejiang Province

Nature Reserve now plays an important part in regulating and purifying the industrial waste gas of Anshan.

The Songhua Lake Nature Reserve in Jilin Province has 420,000 acres of forest and 123,500 acres of lakes. This is a comprehensive ecosystem that provides four major resources—water, energy, and biological and climatic resources—for the nearby industrial cities.

This brief overview covers just a few of the 316 nature reserves occupying 42 million acres, or 1.8 percent of China's total area, but it indicates the importance China places on protecting and developing her precious natural heritage. New reserves are constantly being created in accordance with plans for about 500 nature reserves by the year 2000, including some 330 flora reserves, 130 fauna reserves, and 35 reserves for preserving geological and other sites.

RARE ANIMALS UNDER
GOVERNMENT PROTECTION

A. White-lipped deer (Thorold's deer) *Cervus albirostris* **B.** Pig-tailed macaque *Macaca nemestrina* **C.** Steppe cat *Felis manul*
D. Clouded leopard *Neofelis nebulosa* **E.** Mountain turtle *Trionyx steindachneri* **F.** Malayan soft-shelled turtle *Pelochelys bibroni*
G. Hobby *Falco subbuteo*

A. Black finless porpoise *Neomeris phocoenoides*   **B.** Snow hare *Lepus timidus*   **C.** White stork *Ciconia ciconia*   **D.** Gaur *Bibos gaurus*
E. Serow *Capricornis sumatraensis*   **F.** Green peafowl *Pavo muticus*   **G.** Great bustard *Otis tarda*   **H.** Chinese crocodile lizard *Shinisaurus crocodilurus*   **I.** Mouse deer *Tragulus javanicus*   **J.** Red kite *Milvus milvus*

A. Chinese paddlefish *Psephurus gladius* **B.** Little whimbrel *Numenius borealis* **C.** Assamese macaque *Macaca assamensis* **D.** Silver pheasant *Lophura nycthemera* **E.** Songjiang sculpin *Trachidermus fasciatus* **F.** Derby's parakeet *Psittacula derbiana* **G.** Glutton *Gulo gulo* **H.** Goat *Procapra picticaudata*

A. Binturong *Arctictis binturong* **B.** Beaver *Castor fiber* **C.** Tonkins langur *Presbytis froncisi* **D.** White-naped crane *Grus vipio*
E. Sambar deer *Elaphodus Cephalophus* **F.** Golden cat *Felis temminckii* **G.** Brown owl *Ninox scutulata scutulata* **H.** Ermine *Mustela erminea* **I.** Black-necked crane *Grus nigricollis*

A. Brown-eared pheasant *Crossoptilon manchuricum* **B.** Two-banded monitor *Varanus salvator* **C.** Ibex *Capra ibex* **D.** Chinese copper pheasant *Chrysolophus amherstiae* **E.** Chinese sturgeon *Acipenser sinensis* **F.** Brown wood owl *Strix leptogrammica* **G.** Wild camel *Camelus ferus* **H.** Reindeer *Rangifer tarandus*

A. White-tailed sea eagle *Haliaeetus albicilla*   **B.** Kansu red deer *Cervus elaphus macneilli*   **C.** Mouse deer *Tragulus javanicus*
D. Tibetan wild ass *Equus hemionus kiang*   **E.** Stump-tailed macaque *Macaca speciosa*   **F.** Chinese desert cat *Felis bieti*   **G.** Blood
pheasant *Ithaginis cruentus* **H.** Chinese river deer *Hydropotes inermis*

A. Python *Python molurus* **B.** Red deer *Cervus elaphus* **C.** Chinese merganser *Mergus squamatus* **D.** Long-tailed langur *Presbytis entellus* **E.** Slow loris *Nycticebus coucang* **F.** Tokay *Gekko gecko* **G.** Buzzard *Buteo buteo* **H.** Brown bear *Ursus arctos* **I.** Black gibbon *Hylobates concolor*

A. Lancelet *Branchiostoma belcheri* **B.** Blue eared pheasant *Crossoptilon* **C.** Wild yak *Bos grunniens mutus* **D.** White-crowned long-tailed pheasant *Syrmaticus reevesii* **E.** Goshawk *Accipiter gentilis* **F.** Goitered gazelle *Gazella subgutturosa* **G.** Chinese tragopon *Tragopan temminckii* **H.** Goral *Naemorhedus goral* **I.** Siberian crane *Grus Leucogeranus*

A. Giant salamander *Megalobatrachus davidianus*   **B.** Chinese river dolphin *Lipotes vexillifer*   **C.** Crested shelduck *Tadorna cristata*
D. Eld's deer *Cervus eldi hainanus*   **E.** Himalayan monal pheasant *Lophophorus impejanus*   **F.** Mandarin duck *Aix galericulata*   **G.** Wart
salamander *Tylototriton spp* **H.** Great egret *Egretta alba*

A. Hazel grouse *Tetrastes bonasia* **B.** Chinese pangolin *Manis pentadactyla* **C.** Malabar pied hornbill *Anthracoceros coronatus*

D. Booby *Sula spp* **E.** Red panda *Ailurus fulgens* **F.** Leopard *Panthera pardus* **G.** Mongolian wild ass *Equus hemionus hemionus*

H. Brown-headed gull *Larus brunnicephalus* **I.** Northeast China tiger *Panthera tigris anurensis* **J.** Seal *Phoca vitulina*

A. Snowy owl *Nyctea scandiaca*   **B.** Red stingray *Dasyatis akajei*   **C.** Cape barn owl *Tyto capensis*   **D.** Black stork *Ciconia nigra*
E. Snow leopard *Panthera uncia*   **F.** Tibetan antelope *Pantholops hodgsoni*   **G.** Argali sheep *Ovis ammon*   **H.** Chinese monal *Lophophorus lhuysii*   **I.** Little civet *Viverricula indica*

A. Long-eared owl *Asio otus* **B.** Common otter *Lutra spp* **C.** Koklas pheasant *Pucrasia macrolopha* **D.** Chinese alligator (Yangtze alligator) *Alligator sinensis* **E.** Golden pheasant *Chrysolophus pictus* **F.** Sika deer *Cervus nippon* **G.** Musk deer *Moschus spp* **H.** Asiatic elephant *Elephas maximus* **I.** Spotted-billed pelican *Pelecanus philippensis* **J.** Père David's deer *Elaphurus davidianus*

A. Sable *Martes zibellina*   **B.** Kestrel *Falco tinnunculus*   **C.** Rhesus monkey *Macaca mulatta*   **D.** South China tiger *Panthera tigris amoyensis*   **E.** Cinereous vulture *Aegypius monachus*   **F.** Golden eagle *Aquila chrysaëtos*   **G.** Sarus crane *Grus antigone*   **H.** Horned grebe *Podiceps auritus*   **I.** Fukien tragopan (Cabot's tragopan) *Tragopan caboti*   **J.** Hog deer *Axis porcinus*

A. Great hornbill *Buceros bicornis*   **B.** Red goral *Naemorhedus cranbrooki*   **C.** Capercaillie *Tetrao spp*   **D.** Demoiselle crane *Anthropoides virgo*   **E.** Caped langur *Presbytis pileatus*   **F.** Asian bullfrog *Rana tigerina*   **G.** Turtle *Chelonia mydas*   **H.** White-necked long-tailed pheasant *Syrmaticus ellioti*   **I.** Common crane *Grus grus*

A. Tibetan eared pheasant *Crossoptilon crossoptilon* **B.** Lynx *Felis lynx* **C.** Giant squirrel *Ratufa bicolor*
D. Blyth's tragopan *Trago blythii* **E.** Red-breasted parakeet *Psittacula alexandri* **F.** Golden monkey *Rhinopithecus roxellanae* **G.** Crested ibis *Nipponia nippon* **H.** White-browed gibbon *Hylobates hoolock* **I.** Swan *Cygnus spp*

A. Tufted deer *Elaphodus cephalophus* **B.** Rufous-necked hornbill *Aceros nipalensis* **C.** Lesser blue-winged pitta *Pitta brachyura*

D. Barred owlet *Glaucidium cuculoides* **E.** Kamchatkan sea eagle *Haliaeetus pelagicus* **F.** Hooded crane *Grus monacha*

G. Spoonbill *Platalea leucorodia* **H.** White-handed gibbon *Hylobates lar* **I.** Wild horse *Equus przewalskii*

A. Four-toed tortoise *Testudo horsfieldii*   **B.** Kalij pheasant *Lophura leucomelana*   **C.** White-headed langur *Presbytis leucocephalus*
D. Giant panda *Ailuropoda melanoleuca*   **E.** Taiwan blue pheasant *Lophura swinhoii*   **F.** White ibis *Threskiornis melanocephala*
G. Takin *Budorcas taxicolor*   **H.** Little bustard *Otis tetrax*

RARE PLANTS UNDER
GOVERNMENT PROTECTION

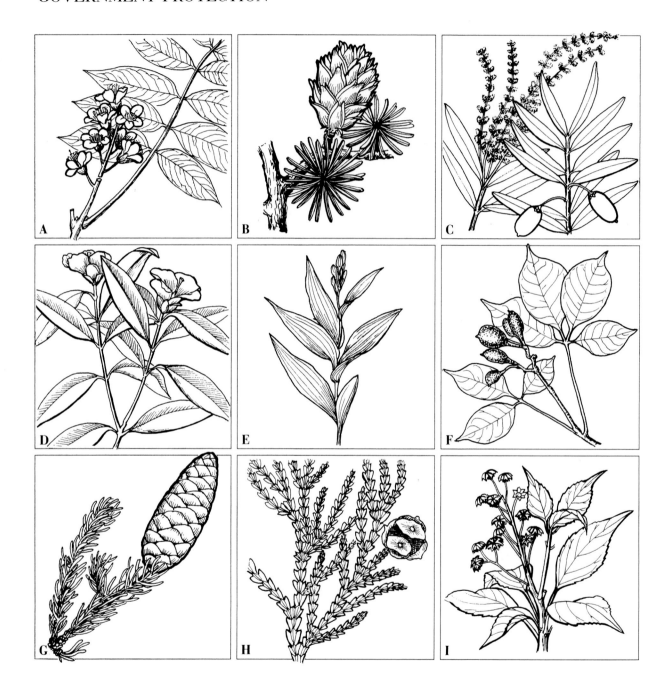

A. *Bretschneidera sinensis* Hemsl. **B.** *Pseudolarix amabilis* (Nelson) Rehd. **C.** *Amentotaxus yunnanensis* Li. **D.** *Mesua ferrea* L.
E. *Tangtsinia nanchuanica* S. C. Chen **F.** *Handeliodendron bodinieri* (Lévl.) Rehd. **G.** *Picea neoveitchii* Mast. **H.** *Fokienia*
hodginsii (Dunn) Henry & Thomas **I.** *Trochodendron aralioides* Sieb. & Zucc.

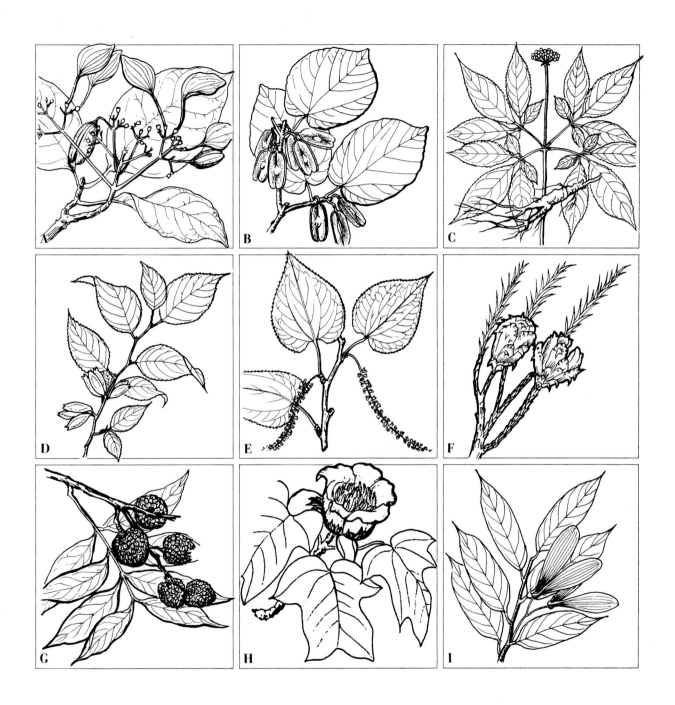

A. *Emmenopterys henryi* Oliv.   **B.** *Burretiodendron esquirolii* (Lévl.) Rehd.   **C.** *Panax ginseng* C. A. Mey.   **D.** *Eucommia ulmoides* Oliv.
E. *Tetracentron sinense* Oliv.   **F.** *Glyptostrobus pensilis* (Staunt.) Koch   **G.** *Litchi chinensis* Sonn.   **H.** *Liriodendron chinense* (Hemsl.)
Sarg.   **I.** *Hopea chinensis* (Merr.) Hand.-Mazz.

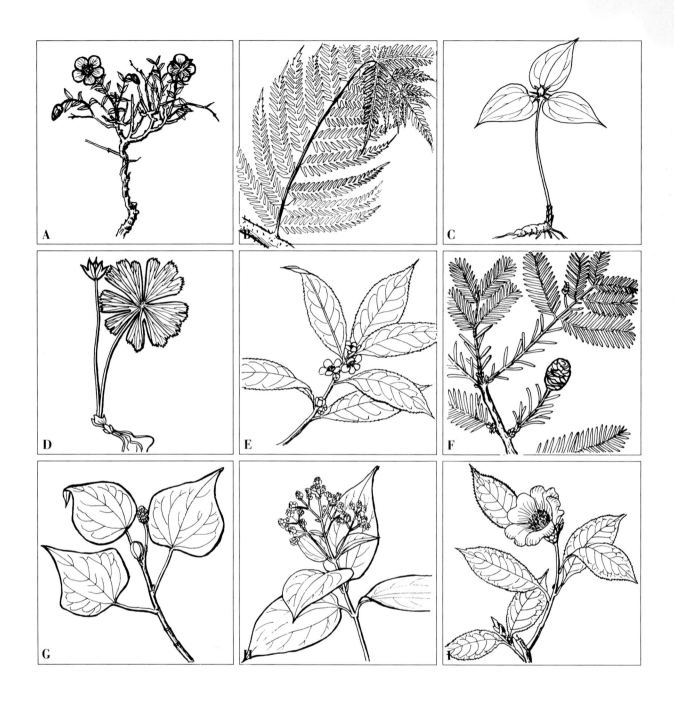

A. *Helianthemum soongaricum* Schrenk B. *Cyathea spinulosa* Wall. C. *Trillium govarianum* Wall. *ex* Royle D. *Kingdonia uniflora* Balf. f. & W. W. Smith E. *Camellia sinensis* var. *assamica* (Mast.) Kitam. F. *Metasequoia glyptostroboides* Hu & Cheng G. *Chunia bucklandioides* H. T. Chang H. *Heptacodium jasminoides* Airy Shaw I. *Camellia grijsii* Hance

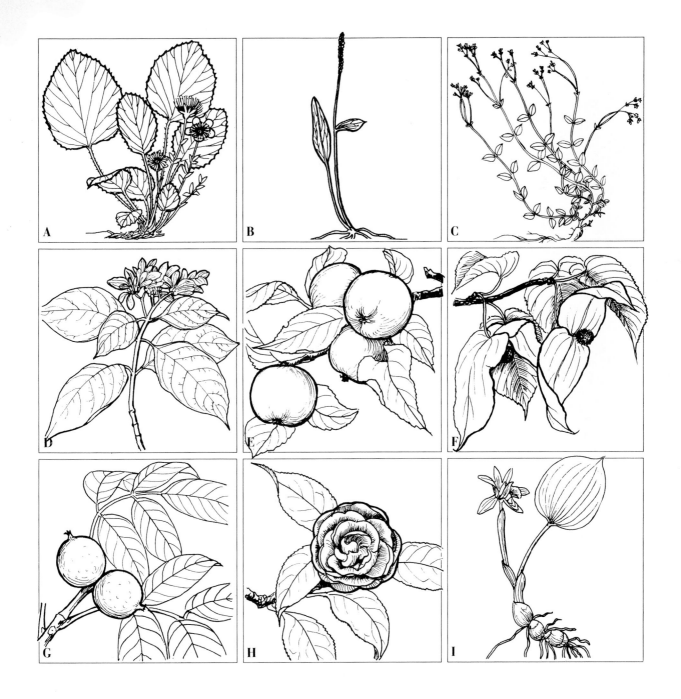

A. *Taihangia rupestris* Yü & Li B. *Merseburg Ruf* C. *Psammosilene tunicoides* W. C. Wu & C. Y. Wu D. *Mussaenda anomala* Li E. *Malus sieversii* (Ledeb.) Roem. F. *Davidia involucrata* Baill. G. *Juglans regia* L. H. *Camellia reticulata* Lindl. I. *Changrienia amoena* Chien

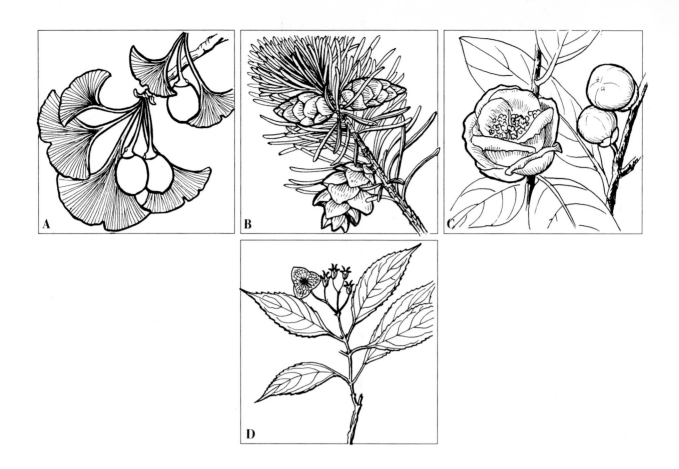

A. *Ginkgo biloba* L. **B.** *Cathaya argyrophylla* Chun & Kuang **C.** *Camellia chrysantha* (Hu) Tuyama **D.** *Platycrater arguta* Sieb. & Zucc.